HISTORY OF THE
GRAND PRIX

HISTORY OF THE GRAND PRIX

Alan Henry

BISON GROUP

First published in 1990 by
Bison Books Ltd
Kimbolton House
117A Fulham Road
London
SW3 6RL

ISBN 0-86124-622-5

Printed in Hong Kong

10 9 8 7 6 5 4 3 2

Reprinted 1992

Page 1: Jim Clark, widely regarded as possibly the greatest driver of all time, seen after winning the 1967 United States Grand Prix at Watkins Glen.

Pages 2-3: The essence of Grand Prix racing in the last year of the turbos. Alain Prost's McLaren-Honda MP4/4 just beats Nigel Mansell's Williams-Judd to the first corner of the Spanish Grand Prix at Jerez, the rest of the pack jostling in their wake.

Below: When the world was young. Duray's Delage (35) and the Sunbeam of Lee-Guinness (36) line up to contest the 1914 Grand Prix de l'ACF.

Contents

Part 1

Early Days

The Pioneering Years

From the very dawn of motoring itself, man's intriguing love affair with the internal combustion engine and the machines it propelled has verged on the obsessive. Spiced with the human competitive spirit, it was only to be expected that cars would be raced with the same spirit, tenacity and commitment as man had hitherto applied to such high risk pastimes as horse racing, hunting and duelling. Thus, as the nineteenth century flickered to its end, the very foundation stones of the spectacle we now know as World Championship Formula 1 Grand Prix motor racing were firmly put in their place.

Few areas of man's endeavour have made progress as dramatic as that achieved in motor racing circles. Not one hundred years have passed since the first motorised reliability run took place between Paris and Rouen, won by Count de Dion in a car bearing his own name. The first 'Grand Prize', as such, did not occur until 1906 when two days racing on a 65-mile road circuit based on Le Mans took place, competitors being required to complete six laps of the route on each day.

The winner, Ferenc Szis, took over eleven hours in total to achieve this success at an average speed just topping 63mph. Had one been able to transport Szis through a time warp into a Grand Prix paddock of the late 1980s, it would surely have been very similar to dropping a cave dweller into the headquarters of the NASA space programme. Disbelief would hardly make a start at describing his feelings . . .

Yet top-line international motor racing has specialised in bringing the unbelievable to life throughout its relatively short life span, technological ingenuity and commercial audacity being a common theme which crops up again and again over the decades. However, the sport's development during those pioneering years tended to be piecemeal and uncoordinated. Between that first Paris-Rouen trial in 1894 and the abandonment of major international road races in 1904, following the tragic Paris-Madrid epic in which many competitors and onlookers were killed, no fewer than thirty four such events took place, a large proportion of which started in Paris.

It is perhaps difficult to imagine the primitive conditions in which these races were run. Roads were little more than pockmarked, dusty, stony tracks with no proper surfacing to speak of; safety facilities, either for competitor or spectator, were non-existent; solid tyres were the norm. The first Paris-Rouen event was won at the modest average of 11.6mph, which must have seemed quite fast enough at the time, while technology had hardly improved spectacularly by the time Felice Nazzaro won the 1907 French Grand Prix, averaging a breathtaking 70.5mph round the 47.8-mile circuit based on Dieppe.

France regarded herself as the cradle of the automobile and seized the initiative when it came to organising international motoring competitions, an historical quirk which has been perpetuated through to contemporary times, accompanied by varying degrees of controversy.

After the carnage of the Paris-Madrid affair, international racing increasingly took place on closed circuits, although they were hardly 'short laps' in the sense that we have got to know them in contemporary times. For example, the Circuit of the Ardennes was inaugurated in 1902 over a 53½-mile closed circuit, Le Mans had a lap length of 65 miles and that year's Gordon Bennett Cup was staged on a closed circuit of Irish public roads with a total lap distance of 103 miles.

The Gordon Bennett Cup races took their name from the US

Previous page: Felice Nazzaro's Fiat storms away from the first ever massed start at the 1922 Grand Prix de l'ACF at Strasbourg.

Above: Suicide alley. The 1903 Paris-Madrid event hardly took much account of spectator safety – and the photographers were arguably braver, or had less imagination, than the drivers!

Near left: Henri Farman's Panhard contested the 1902 Paris-Vienna race and won the 'heavy car' category.

Far left: Charles Jarrot's fearsome de Dietrich at Bordeaux during the epic 1903 Paris-Madrid road race.

Right: Gabriel's Mors kicks up the dust in the same event, much to the fascination of the ladies on the right. Rather overdressed for Brands Hatch perhaps?

Left: Callan's Wolsley contesting the 1903 Circuit des Ardennes, a modestly short event compared with the city-to-city classics.

Right: Early days of a great name as de Caters' Mercedes contests the 1903 Gordon Bennett Cup contest.

Below: Théry's Richard Brasier fighting for Gordon Bennett Cup honours, 1904.

newspaper magnate who initiated the concept of a competition involving three car teams from each participating country. This series attracted a great deal of attention and publicity during the early years of the century, but it was an extremely uncertain time from the viewpoint of codified technical regulations which would bring some semblance of order to what was fast developing into a 'free formula'.

By 1907, the concept of a Grand Prix formula was becoming established, at this early stage based round a fuel consumption restriction with 30 litres per 100km permitted. However, the following year the regulations were altered, now based on a piston area restriction, producing a breed of four-cylinder cars with short-stroke, push-rod, overhead valve engines, typically developing from 130-140bhp from a massive 12-litre cubic capacity.

The Grand Prix category was effectively abandoned between 1909-11, newly established firms such as Peugeot and Delage concentrating on the 'voiturette' category for 'small-engined' (300cc) cars, but by 1913 the Grand Prix category had been revitalised running under a 14mpg fuel consumption limit.

In 1912, Swiss engineer Ernest Henry, who was employed by Peugeot, produced a cylinder head layout which has remained basically unchanged for high performance engines to this day. Incorporating four valves per cylinder, it had two overhead camshafts which operated inclined valves in hemispherical combustion chambers.

The First World War then intervened, but not before Mercedes finished first, second and third in the final French Grand Prix to be held prior to the commencement of hostilities. Motor racing was henceforward confined to the USA for the duration, and, in fact, it was not until 1921 that the sport struggled back into life in the European arena which had been so decimated by the rigours of the first of two Anglo-German conflicts not to be confined to the race track.

International racing was now revived under a 3-litre capacity limit, although in 1922 this was reduced to 2-litres and the category endured for another four seasons. The 1922 season also saw the world's first purpose-built circuit constructed, in the former royal park at Monza, near Milan, while the first 'grid' start was staged in the Grand Prix de l'ACF at Strasbourg. Grand Prix racing was now poised to evolve into the sport we are familiar with in the last decade of the twentieth century.

The Early Heroes

Throughout the 1920s and 30s, at least prior to the arrival of the 'Silver Arrows', international motor racing was in a state of constant flux, evolving on several fronts as a series of specialist companies made great strides in engine, chassis and suspension development.

As far as venues were concerned, a succession of new circuits sprang up across Europe, including such historic locations as Monaco which hosted its first race in 1929 when the winner was the Bugatti-mounted William Grover Williams, later to be killed by the Nazis whilst spying for the Allies during the Second World War, as was fellow racer Robert Benoist who had won the 1927 French, Spanish and European Grands Prix at the wheel of a Delage.

The Mercedes which had defeated the Henry-designed Peugeots before the war were hauled out to do business again in the early 1920s, winning the 1922 Targa Florio road race in Sicily. But Jimmy Murphy's Duesenberg won the 1921 Grand Prix de l'ACF to display the efficiency of hydraulic brakes, and Ernest Henry's 1924 2-litre Sunbeam made significant strides in the development of the supercharger.

The number of manufacturers was thinning out slightly by the mid 1920s, such names as Brasier, Clement-Bayard and de Dietrich having gone the way of all flesh, and a scan down the list of international race results during the late 1920s and early 30s reveals that three marques had gained a position of pre-eminence. They were Bugatti, Maserati and Alfa Romeo.

Jules Goux gave the patriarchal Ettore Bugatti his first major international victory in the 1926 French Grand Prix after which the French team's fortunes were carried largely by the debonair Louis Chiron , Achille Varzi and the impish Rene Dreyfus. The French team reached the zenith of its achievement with the T35 which won three races in 1933 in the hands of Frenchman Marcel Lehoux.

The great Italian designer Vittorio Jano really made his mark in the early 1920s with the splendid supercharged, eight cylinder Alfa Romeo P2 which dominated the latter part of the 2-litre formula up to 1925. It gave way to the splendid P3 Alfa Romeo single seater, its eight-cylinder engine now fitted with twin superchargers, which would carry Nuvolari to that historic victory over Mercedes and Auto Union at the Nurburgring in 1935.

Italian dictator Benito Mussolini had already concluded that international motor racing would provide a suitable stage on

Above: Jimmy Murphy's Duesenberg scored a first for hydraulic brakes when he won the 1921 Grand Prix de l'ACF.

Left: Ettore Bugatti at the wheel of one of his early products. Usually he left the driving to his hired hands.

Above right: De Palma's Ballot and Murphy's Duesenberg battling in the 1921 Grand Prix de l'ACF on a rutted, pock-marked dirt surface.

Right: Farina's Maserati, Shuttleworth's Alfa Romeo and Wimille's T35 Bugatti in close company during the 1935 Dieppe Grand Prix. They finished in reverse order to that shown in the photograph – fifth, fourth and Wimille third.

which to display his country's sporting prowess, and the onset of the 750kg regulations for 1934 was seen as offering a splendid chance for the P3 Alfa Romeo and the 2.9-litre Maserati. Mussolini, however, had reckoned without the intervention of Auto Union and Mercedes-Benz, by now backed in terms of morale and cash, by his old pal Adolf Hitler. The net result was the domination of the 1934-39 period by the two great German teams, leaving the Italians to pick up whatever crumbs of success were dropped from the table.

Meanwhile, international motor racing sustained a thriving single seater 'second division' in the form of the 'voiturette' category for 1100cc or 1500cc engines. During the early 1930s Bugatti and Alfa Romeo competed happily in this category along with the British ERAs, the cars inspired by Raymond Mays which would lead to his involvement in the BRM project after the Second World War. As we will see, it was into this category that Enzo Ferrari plunged Alfa Romeo, resulting in the production of the Alfa Romeo 158 which would wreak such havoc against the featherweight opposition existing in the immediate post-Second World War years.

The tragedy of the 1939-45 period in motor racing terms was not simply confined to races lost, but the fact that a generation of Grand Prix drivers missed what would otherwise have been the prime of their career. France's Jean-Pierre Wimille, for example, was in his early forties by the end of the war, as were Louis Chiron, Achille Varzi and Rudolf Caracciola. Similarly, Fangio very nearly missed the boat, being 38 when he arrived on the European scene.

Other casualties of the war years included Bugatti, which was soon to plunge into dire financial straits as a prelude to mid-1950s oblivion, and ERA, which was now but a memory, swept aside in the euphoria surrounding the new BRM, although its solid and trusty products raced on to outlive their manufacturer by many decades.

Above left: Auto Union was quick to put its speed record successes to good promotional use as this advertisement reminds us. Note, however, no mention of driver Hans Stuck's identity.

Left: The impressive frontal aspect of the fearsome 1936 Auto Union.

Right: Achille Varzi, the great Italian hero whose career was truncated by drug addiction.

Far right: Many regarded Tazio Nuvolari as the greatest of all time, but he was to cut a tragic figure as the years advanced.

Nuvolari and the Titans

To the end of his long life, Enzo Ferrari would hold up Tazio Nuvolari as the benchmark by which he judged the performance of other racing drivers he had known and with whom he had worked. To say a driver 'was like Nuvolari' was to confer an enormous compliment, implying that he had bravery, commitment and tenacity laced with an inbred virtuoso driving talent. And yet there was even more to it than that.

The mild-mannered, physically slight Nuvolari seemed to be willed on not simply by the powerhouse of ambition. He was a slave to motor racing as surely as the great Achille Varzi, his contemporary and great rival, became addicted to morphia. The desire and a compelling need to compete drove Nuvolari fearlessly on, pushing him to keep racing long after common sense and prudent judgement should have dictated his retirement.

Born on 18 November 1892 near Mantua, Nuvolari initially made his living as a motorcycle rider, but his aim was to go car racing as soon as the opportunity presented itself. In 1925, he was given the chance to test an Alfa Romeo P2 at Monza, but crashed heavily and was badly injured. Undaunted, a few weeks later he instructed the doctors to strap him up in the optimum position to ride a Bianchi, and then proceeded to win the Italian motorcycle Grand Prix in this precarious state.

In 1930 he joined the Alfa Romeo team alongside the debonair Achille Varzi, successfully duping his compatriot into losing the legendary Mille Miglia road race by closing unobtrusively on to the tail of his car with his own headlights switched off. Shortly before the finish line, he pulled out and overtook the astonished Varzi to score a memorable victory.

In 1931, Nuvolari continued to enjoy considerable success, winning such epic races as the Targa Florio and Italian Grand Prix in the Vittorio Jano-designed Alfa 8C and, in '32, continued his winning ways in the magnificent new Type B Monoposto, popularly known as the P3.

At the start of the 1933 season, the Alfa Romeo factory team withdrew from international racing, entrusting its effort to Enzo Ferrari's own enterprising Scuderia. However, much to Nuvolari's annoyance, the factory did not bequeath the P3s to the Scuderia Ferrari. Nuvolari nonetheless continued to drive for Ferrari, but when his real hopes of making the big time finally came in 1935, and it looked as though he might get a drive in one of the fearsome central-engined Auto Unions, he found his earlier trick on Varzi rather blowing up in his face.

Varzi had beaten him into the Auto Union ranks and, along with the German driver Hans Stuck, conspired to keep Nuvolari out of the team. So it was back to the Scuderia Ferrari where subtle pressure from no less a personality than Fascist dictator Benito Mussolini ensured that the private team now had some Alfa Romeo P3s at its disposal. That 1935 season produced an absolutely classic victory at the Nurburgring when Nuvolari dodged every hazard to keep out of trouble, winning in front of

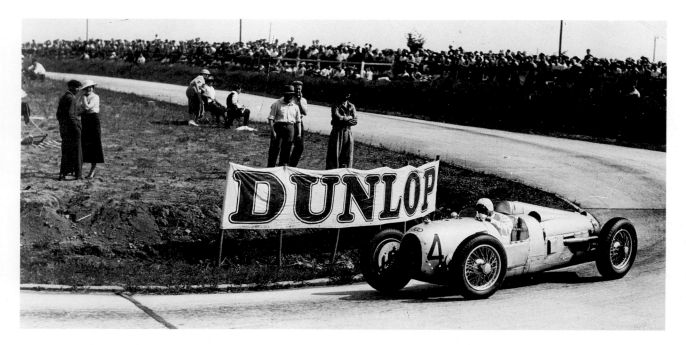

Left: Hans Stuck's Auto Union led the 1934 French Grand Prix at Montlhery before overheating problems forced his retirement.

Below: Nuvolari's tiny frame behind the wheel of the V12 3-litre Auto Union on his way to victory in the 1938 Donington Grand Prix.

Below right: The Mercedes W125 of Dick Seaman leads the 6-litre Auto Unions of legendary Bernd Rosemeyer and his team-mate H. P. Muller in the 1937 Donington Grand Prix. Rosemeyer eventually went ahead to win superbly, the last success of his tragically brief career.

an embarrassed and rather silent crowd after the Mercedes of Manfred von Brauchitsch lost a wheel on the final lap, handing victory to the Italian interloper.

In 1936, Nuvolari stayed loyal to Ferrari, but no major wins came his way, but the long-awaited second approach from one of the two major German teams came in 1937 and he duly joined Auto Union for the '38 season, even though his lingering hopes for Jano's new V12-engined Alfa kept him in two minds right up to the last minute.

The sight of this small man powering the huge, unwieldy silver Auto Union from lock to lock with an air of unconcerned detachment on his face was a treat which European race fans relished for little more than a season. In '38 Nuvolari won not only the Italian Grand Prix at Monza, but also the second Donington Grand Prix, the previous year's event having been won by his predecessor Bernd Rosemeyer, the young genius who was subsequently killed in a speed record attempt on a German autobahn in January 1938.

The final race of 1939 was the Yugoslavian Grand Prix in Belgrade, held in the late afternoon of 3 September, by which time the Second World War was already a few hours old. It was

almost symbolic that Nuvolari emerged triumphant from this event which rounded off a golden, heroic era of European motor racing. Yet when racing resumed in the austere post-war years, Nuvolari would still be there, plodding away. But now he was well over fifty, beset by bronchial problems and a shadow of the man he once was.

He cut a tragic figure. Both his sons died in their prime, tragedies which perhaps forced Nuvolari to overcome by racing as much as he could. Enzo Ferrari admits in his memoirs that, watching Nuvolari come through Modena in the 1947 Mille Miglia, he turned aside and wept. In pouring rain, he was leading the epic road race in a tiny 1500cc Cisitalia, a roller skate of a car. Despite losing time when its engine was virtually swamped, he continued to finish second behind Clemente Biondetti's 3-litre Alfa Romeo. In 1948, he renewed his partnership with Enzo Ferrari, driving one of his new V12-engined machines in the Mille Miglia, again leading until the chassis started to fail.

Tazio Nuvolari struggled on, almost driven by a death wish, to race into 1950, by which time he was 58 years old and very frail. He would die in bed on August 11, 1953, denied his hope that final release would come behind the wheel of a racing car.

The Silver Arrows

The battle for domination which raged between the prestigious German teams, Mercedes-Benz and Auto Union, began in 1934 and was brought to a close not by the arrival on the scene of any superior rival, but by the outbreak of the Second World War. The rise to glory of these German cars, driven not only by the finest crop of home-grown talent, but also the best that Britain and Italy could offer, was seized on by Adolf Hitler's Nazi party as a highly effective medium by which the competitive excellence of the Third Reich could be projected across the world at large.

It did not take long for the contemporary press to name these elegant, imposing and fearsomely powerful racing cars the 'Silberpfelle' – the 'Silver Arrows' – although, while the Auto Unions were always intended to race with polished aluminum bodywork, Mercedes had planned to field its cars in the traditional white livery which had been the manufacturer's hallmark in years gone by. But the technical regulations in force at the time of their 1934 debut, while not placing any restriction on engine capacity, required that the cars should weigh in between 546 and 750kg.

While being officially weighed prior to their debut in the 1934

Eifel Grand Prix at the Nurburgring, the straight-eight cylinder, 3.4-litre supercharged Mercedes W25s were found to be a fraction over the maximum weight limit, much to the consternation of team manager Alfred Neubauer. A chance remark from team driver Manfred von Brauchitsch gave Neubauer the idea of stripping off the cars' white paint overnight, a ploy which worked splendidly to bring the cars just inside the weight limit in time for the race. Appropriately, perhaps, the aristocratic von Brauchitsch won this debut race the following day.

Ranged against the supercharged Mercedes, Auto Union's chief designer Professor Ferdinand Porsche, who would later give his name to one of the most famous of all post-war sports car manufacturers, designed a striking and radically different machine. The 4.4-litre, V16 cylinder rear-engined Auto Union initially developed 295bhp, about 20bhp less than its rival German contender. It was Professor Porsche who originally persuaded Hitler to split the state subsidy for a national Grand Prix effort (in the region of £600,000), all of which was originally earmarked for the established Mercedes company, between it and Auto Union, newcomers to the scene.

Over the years that followed, the 'Silver Arrows' would make

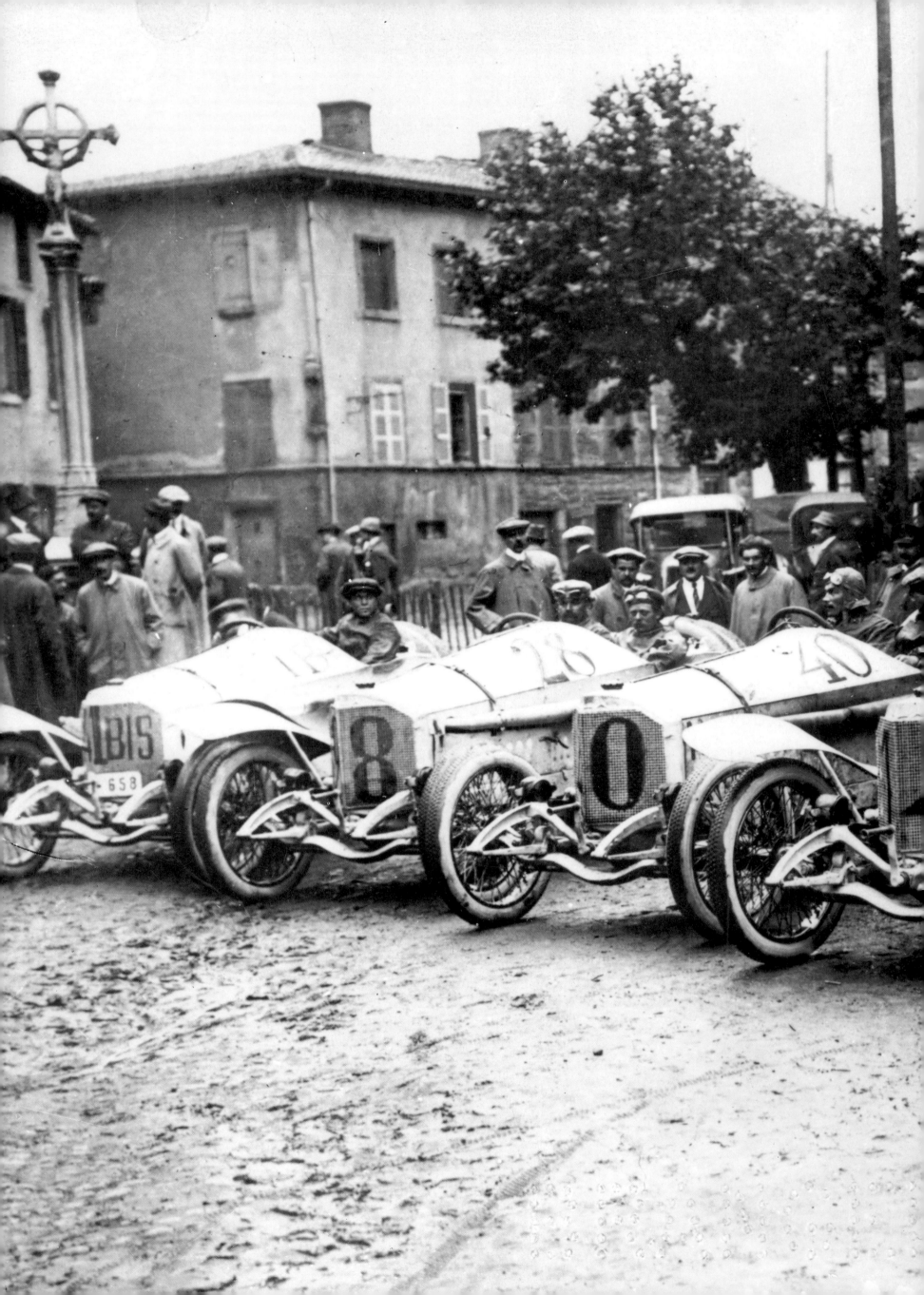

the European Grand Prix scene their own private battle ground,
the Mercedes straight-eight growing in capacity to 3.7 litres,
thence to 4.3 litres and finally, by 1936, to 4.7 litres at which
point it was developing 490bhp. During the same period, the
Auto Union V16 grew spectacularly to 6 litres, by which point it
had overtaken the Mercedes to develop a shattering 520bhp.

This was the sort of power output achieved by Ferrari's 3-litre
flat-12 some forty years later, but with archaic levels of chassis
construction, tyre technology and provision for driver safety.
Yet the Silver Arrows, for all their bulk and comparatively
crude engineering, would touch 200mph on the straight, and
write a chapter in the motor racing history books as being
among the most spectacular racing cars of all time, perhaps only
eclipsed by the unrestricted boost turbo cars of the mid 1980s.

Bugatti, Alfa Romeo and Maserati provided the supporting
cast for this German technical tour-de-force, but a scan through
the results for that momentous five year period reveals precious
little to interrupt the record of silver success. The brilliant Tazio
Nuvolari, of course, would take his Alfa P3 to a superb win in the
'35 German Grand Prix, but only after von Brauchitsch's Mercedes suffered a puncture mid-way round its final lap of the Nurburgring. Nuvolari would remain a persistent thorn in the side
of the German cars through 1936, beating them at Barcelona,
Budapest, Milan and Livorno, while Pat Fairfield's ERA won
the 1937 South African Grand Prix at East London. France's
Rene Dreyfus also did a superb job for Delahaye in fighting off a
Mercedes shared by Rudi Caracciola and Hermann Lang at Pau
in 1938, but such surges against the prevailing tide were the ex-
ception rather than the rule.

As far as Mercedes-Benz was concerned, their greatest ex-
ponent was undoubtedly Rudolf Caracciola. Although he started
the era on a catastrophic note, being invalided out of the team
for over a season after badly breaking his right thigh and hip in
practice for the 1934 Monaco Grand Prix, he would bounce back
to win three European Championships and 15 Grands Prix
before the Second World War.

Among his team-mates would be Manfred von Brauchitsch
and Italian Luigi Fagioli, who came from a humble background
and was regarded with disdain by the aristocratic German
whose uncle would become commander-in-chief of the German

Army in 1938, rising to the rank of field marshal. Over at Auto Union, the debonair Achille Varzi shone brilliantly as a team member in 1935 and 36 before falling victim to drug addiction, wrecking his career as a top class driver.

In 1937, Mercedes-Benz unveiled its breathtaking W125, its straight-eight engine now enlarged to 5.6-litres and developing 580bhp. Together with the 6-litre Auto Unions, they produced a breathtaking finale to the 750kg formula, with the dazzlingly talented young former motorcycle racer, Bernd Rosemeyer, coming into his own to handle the fearsome rear-engined beast with a spectacular bravery and skill that many regarded as unmatched, even by Tazio Nuvolari who raced through to the end of 1939 with Auto Union.

Tragically, Rosemeyer would be killed in a record attempt on a German autobahn in the early weeks of 1938, not surviving to drive the 3-litre supercharged V12-engined Auto Union which would do battle with a similarly-powered Mercedes during the final two seasons remaining before war broke out.

In 1937, Mercedes also signed up the young Englishman Dick Seaman who had made such an impression at the wheel of both an ERA and the ten year old, ex-Earl Howe, Delage during the previous season. Seaman was destined to become Britain's first truly world-class international Grand Prix driver and catapulted to prominence with a politically rather tense victory in the 1938 German Grand Prix. However at the age of 26 he died of burns sustained when his Mercedes crashed while leading the 1939 Belgian Grand Prix at Spa. The race was won by his Mercedes team-mate Hermann Lang, who also went on to clinch the 1939 European Championship.

It had been an era where inbred class snobbery among the drivers was inextricably interwoven with intense rivalry and technical excellence, as witness the occasion on which Manfred von Brauchitsch led Hermann Lang and Rudi Caracciola into a restaurant. Summoning a waiter he barked out an order which perfectly captured the flavour of the time.

'A bottle of champagne, if you please, for myself and Herr Caracciola,' adding, as an afterthought, 'And a beer for Lang . . .'

Above left: Bernd Rosemeyer, one of the most glamorous and admired young German sportsmen of his day. Rosemeyer crashed fatally in a record attempt early in 1938. He was just 27.

Left: Rosemeyer in classic pose behind the wheel of the Porsche-designed Auto Union.

Above right: Rosemeyer captivated the Donington Park crowds with his magical car control at the wheel of the Auto Union in 1937.

Right: Hermann Lang's Mercedes W154 in the 1939 French Grand Prix at Reims. Lang became the last European Champion before the continent was engulfed in war.

Part 2
The 1950s

Alfa Romeo's Post-war Momentum

As Europe began to pick up the pieces following the devastation wrought by the Second World War, so the motor racing fraternity picked up the threads which had been so brutally severed in September 1939. Initially, of course, resources were far too scarce for anybody to contemplate building new racing cars, so pre-war machines which had been stored away for the duration were now retrieved, dusted down and then coaxed into hesitant action.

The most celebrated of all these throw-backs to the pre-war era were Alfa Romeo's straight-eight cylinder, supercharged 1½-litre Tipo 158s, machines which would become popularly dubbed 'Alfettas'. Conceived by Giacchino Colombo during Enzo Ferrari's tenure as Alfa Romeo racing manager in the mid 1930s, based round tubular frames with trailing arm front suspension and swing-axles at the rear, the type 158s, were designed in conformity with the technical regulations for the 'voiturette' class, then effectively a 'second division' of international single seater racing. Alfa Romeo also had in mind the proposed 1½-litre supercharged/4½-litre unsupercharged Grand Prix rules which the sport's international governing body, the Alliance Internationale des Automobiles Reconnus (AIACR) had outlined for 1941 and the engine was, in essence, a single bank of a planned V16 design prepared for the pre-war 3-litre supercharged/4½-litre unsupercharged category.

The proposed 1941 regulations were subsequently resurrected to govern Formula 1 in the immediate post-war era and a trio of Alfa 158s was duly retrieved from secret storage in a cheese factory to take part. The cars had originally made their debut in the 1938 Coppa Ciano at Leghorn, where they finished first and second, and their post-war reappearance came eight years later in the Grands Prix des Nations at Geneva where they were driven by Nino Farina, Count Trossi and Jean-Pierre Wimille.

Between 1946 and 48, the 158s were well capable of dealing with the makeweight opposition, in the form of the plodding 4½-litre Talbots, pre-war Maserati 4CLs and similarly ageing ERAs. Alfa took a year off in 1949, but were back to contest the first official World Championship in 1950. By then, Wimille, Achille Varzi and Count Trossi were all dead, so the 158s were driven by Farina, 38-year old Argentine newcomer Juan Manuel Fangio and Luigi Fagioli.

The first title battle was fought out over six races with the best four to count, points being awarded on an 8-6-4-3-2 basis for the top five finishers. The season commenced with the British Grand Prix at Silverstone where, under the royal patronage of King George VI and Queen Elizabeth, Farina, Fagioli and English nominee Reg Parnell finished in 1-2-3 formation with little in the way of serious opposition.

However, while Enzo Ferrari's newly established company was laying a firm F1 footing for the future, developing a naturally aspirated machine in addition to its 1½-litre V12-

Previous page: Juan Manuel Fangio won his fifth World Championship with the elegant Maserati 250F, seen here in the 1957 British Grand Prix at Aintree.

Left: Fangio started his European campaign during 1948/49 in a Maserati entered by the Argentine Automobile Club.

Above right: Nino Farina, seen here with an Alfa 158 in the Grand Prix des Nations at Geneva, won the first official World Championship in 1950.

Near right: Alberto Ascari was Champion for Ferrari in 1952 and 53.

Far right: Fangio in the cockpit of his Maserati, circa 1949.

Above: Fangio's Alfa 159 leads away at the start of the 1951 French Grand Prix at Reims pursued by Ascari's Ferrari 375 (12), Gonzalez's similar car (10) and the Alfas of Villoresi (2) and Farina (6).

Left: Fangio on his way to second place in the 1951 British Grand Prix where his Alfa 159 was beaten by Froilan Gonzalez in the Ferrari 375.

engined cars driven by Alberto Ascari and Luigi Villoresi, Alfa Romeo had the stage to itself throughout 1950. Farina would also triumph in the Swiss Grand Prix at Berne and the Italian Grand Prix at Monza, leaving Fangio to win at Monaco, Spa and Reims. Farina emerged World Champion with 30 points, three more than Fangio, with Fagioli third on 24.

Meanwhile, Ferrari engineer Aurelio Lampredi was really cracking on with the development of a full 4.5-litre naturally aspirated V12, the 'other' Italian team realising that it would be quite possible to beat the Alfas by the simple expedient of making fewer pit stops than the 158s.

The 1951 season would mark the golden swansong of the Alfa straight-eights, now heavily revised and designated Tipo 159s. The output of their supercharged engines had now been boosted to 404bhp at 9500rpm, over twice the 190bhp claimed output with which they had raced immediately before the war, but consumption of alcohol-laced fuel was now down to a crippling 1½ mpg which meant that the 70 gallon fuel load represented almost one fifth of the car's all-up weight of around one ton at the start of a race.

Alfa successfully avoided its new Ferrari opposition in the non-championship pre-season skirmishes, three of which, at Syracuse, Pau and San Remo, fell to Ascari in the new 4.5-litre Ferrari 375. Alfa Romeo's record remained intact in the rain-soaked Swiss Grand Prix, but Piero Taruffi's Ferrari had led off

the line and eventually finished second to Fangio's winning Alfa. The writing was now very firmly on the wall.

The theoretical Ferrari advantage was negated in the Belgian Grand Prix at Spa where a scheduled single stop apiece for both their own 375s and the Alfa 159s produced a commanding three minute victory for Farina with Ascari and Villoresi second and third. Fangio had taken the lead from the start, but the Argentinian lost all prospect of victory when a wheel jammed on its hub during a routine pit stop.

Alfa was now fighting with its back hard against the wall and, after Ascari shared second place for Ferrari in the French Grand Prix at Reims with Argentina's Froilan Gonzalez, Alfa Romeo finally met their Waterloo in the British Grand Prix at Silverstone. There the stocky Gonzalez, whose bulk almost overhung the Ferrari's cockpit, played a superb game of cat and mouse with the more powerful, but heavier Alfa 159s. At the end of the two hour race he was firmly ahead of Fangio.

Once breached, Alfa Romeo's ramparts were quickly overwhelmed by Maranello. Ascari followed up Gonzalez's success by beating the 159s at Nurburgring and Monza, but Fangio's victory in the Spanish Grand Prix at Barcelona secured him the first of his five World Championship titles. Ferrari and Fangio may have been in the ascendant, but for Alfa Romeo it was the end of an era which had begun 14 years earlier in a very different world and the 159s did not race again.

Ferrari's Foundation Stone

Enzo Ferrari made his name operating what was in effect the Alfa Romeo factory team from 1929 to 38, but fell out with the company after a major policy disagreement with director Ugo Gobbato over the strategy that should be adopted towards the racing programme. These problems were aggravated when Alfa Romeo recruited the Spanish engineer Wilfredo Ricart to whom Enzo Ferrari took an instant and enduring dislike.

The nub of Ferrari's problem was Alfa Romeo's avowed intention to re-enter racing as a factory team, effectively absorbing the Scuderia Ferrari and transferring it from its existing base at Modena to Alfa's headquarters at Portello in Milan. This was not an arrangement calculated to suit the ambitious, independent-minded Enzo who parted company with Alfa Romeo the following year, bound by a severance clause forbidding his participation in any racing, unless with an Alfa Romeo car, for the next four years.

Yet, by the end of 1940, he had formed a new company – Auto Avio Construzioni – which would build a couple of eight cylinder sports cars which were simply dubbed 'Tipo 815s'. In reality they

were the first Ferraris and, in 1943, Enzo moved his base from the Scuderia Ferrari premises in central Modena out to a new site at a village called Maranello where he built a new factory on a piece of land he already owned.

Two of the very first Ferrari 125, 1.5-litre V12-engined sports cars made their racing debut at Piacenza on 11 May 1947 in the hands of Nino Farina and Franco Cortese, but the marque first competed in a Formula 1 Grand Prix at Monaco on 16 May 1948. There, Count Igor Troubetskoy, later to gain fame as one of Woolworth heir Barbara Hutton's many husbands, entered a 2-litre type 166 Ferrari sports car. He failed to finish, crashing without injury at the chicane.

On 4 September 1948, the first of the supercharged Ferrari 125 Grand Prix cars made its race debut in the hands of Farina, Raymond Sommer and Prince Bira in the Turin Grand Prix. Designed by former Alfa 158 designer Gioacchino Colombo, with whom Enzo Ferrari had worked during his time with the rival Italian team, it was fitted with a single Weber 50WCF caburetter and a single-stage Roots-type supercharger, the V12 engine

developing 225bhp at 7000rpm. On its maiden outing, Sommer proved the sole survivor, finishing third behind Wimille's victorious Alfa 158 and Villoresi's Maserati.

For 1949, Ferrari concentrated on developing the 125 concept, supplementing his company's income by selling two such machines, one to privateer Peter Whitehead, the other to British engine-bearing magnate Tony Vandervell. Ironically, this latter machine, dubbed the 'Thinwall Special', would be used as a competition test bed for Vandervell thinwall bearings, the first brick in the foundations of the Vanwall Grand Prix team which would beat the Ferraris to the Constructors' World Championship some ten years hence.

Ferrari's first major international Grand Prix success eventually came in the 1949 Swiss Grand Prix at Berne's spectacular Bremgarten circuit. Alberto Ascari and Luigi Villoresi finished first and second in their supercharged 125s, an outcome undoubtedly helped by the fact that Alfa Romeo chose to absent itself from the racing scene throughout that season. By the end of the season Maranello's two-stage supercharged version of the V12 Tipo 125 was developing around 300bhp, but rumours abounded that the Alfa straight-eight, scheduled to return to the scene the following year, was now pushing out in excess of 330bhp. It was time for a change of technical emphasis.

By the end of 1949, Colombo's role as senior engineer had been taken by the imaginative 32-year old Aurelio Lampredi who concluded that the 4½-litre non-supercharged option would be the best route to follow, particularly bearing in mind that the current formula was set to continue through to the end of 1953.

Left: Early days: Enzo Ferrari (far right) is seen at Monza in 1923 with Giorgio Rimini and the debonair Nicola Romeo.

Above: Fangio's burly compatriot Froilan Gonzalez was the man who broke the Alfa stranglehold with Ferrari's victory in the '51 British Grand Prix.

Right: Raymond Sommer leads for Ferrari in the 1948 Gran Premio d'Italia in the rain at Turin's Valentino Park.

Left: Hunched over the wheel of his Ferrari 375, Gonzalez heads to that historic first Ferrari World Championship Grand Prix victory at Silverstone.

Right: Two views of the magnificent 2-litre Ferrari 500 of the type used by Ascari to win the 1952 and 53 World Championships when Formula 2 regulations were in force.

Thus, while Ferrari raced the supercharged 125s from the start of the 1950 season, Lampredi went ahead and developed his naturally aspirated 60-degree V12 concept which duly made its race debut in interim 3.3-litre form, developing 280bhp at 7000rpm, in the 1950 Belgian Grand Prix.

Ascari drove the new car to fifth place on its debut, but it was withdrawn from the French Grand Prix at Reims after proving disappointingly slow in practice. With a further enlarged 4.1-litre V12 installed in a new chassis, with de Dion rear suspension and a new four-speed gearbox in unit with the final drive, for the Grand Prix des Nations at Geneva, its prospects were revitalised. Now it developed 320bhp at 7000rpm and the metamorphosis was finally completed in time for the Italian Grand Prix at Monza where the fully developed, 80 x 74.5mm, 4.44-litre V12 appeared, developing 330bhp.

Although significantly more fuel efficient than the Alfa straight-eights, Lampredi made a big effort to coax even more power out of Ferrari's V12 in time for the 1951 season. With twin-plug ignition and a higher compression ratio, the Ferrari Tipo 375s now produced 380bhp at 7500rpm and it was clearly only a matter of time before Alfa's domination succumbed.

For 1951, Ascari and Villoresi were retained with Piero Taruffi dovetailing as many races as possible with his duties as the Gilera motorcycle Grand Prix team's chief engineer. The demands of this work were responsible for introducing Jose Froilan Gonzalez, a spectacular, energetic and rotund Argentinian driver to the European scene. Gonzalez had made his name by driving a 2-litre supercharged Ferrari to victory over the trio of 1939 Mercedes-Benz W163s which had been sent to Argentina to contest the Peron and Eva Peron Cups at Buenos Aires' Costanera circuit early in 1951.

Nicknamed the Pampas Bull, a soubriquet which aptly reflected the frantic state he seemed to work himself up into whenever he was behind the wheel, Gonzalez would go forward to take an honoured place in Ferrari history as the man who won

the marque its historic first World Championship Grand Prix victory.

Gonzalez made his debut with the factory team at Reims, taking the place of Taruffi, who was unwell, for the French Grand Prix. After Ascari's Ferrari 375 wilted with magneto trouble after a mere nine laps' battling against Fangio's Alfa 159, the Italian would subsequently commandeer Gonzalez's sister car to finish second. Yet when the same situation threatened to rear its head a fortnight later, in the British Grand Prix at Silverstone, Ascari generously insisted Gonzalez should stay in his car.

Having qualified on pole position, Gonzalez had been the fastest Ferrari driver all afternoon, consolidating an early lead on a circuit where the straights were just not long enough for the Alfa 159s to get into their stride. Racing grimly against Fangio, his compatriot, Gonzalez gave it his all, arms flailing dramatically, his bulk brimming over the sides of the cockpit.

On lap 56 Ascari's 375 retired with gearbox problems and, four laps later, when Gonzalez arrived at his final refuelling stop he began to lift himself from the cockpit, obviously assuming that the great Alberto would exercise his prerogative as senior driver and take over for the run to the finish. Ascari merely smiled and placed a reassuring hand on his shoulder, indicating that he should stay behind the wheel.

It was a grand gesture. Gonzalez accelerated back into the race and eventually beat Fangio's Alfa 159 by 50 seconds at the chequered flag. Breaking the mould in which Grand Prix racing had been cast since 1946, Gonzalez's triumph represented a very personal success for Enzo Ferrari who now felt that he had got even with his former employers after all those years.

In the wake of this success, Ferrari fired off an emotional telegram to the Alfa Romeo management which included the phrase, 'I still feel for our Alfa the adolescent tenderness of first love.' But it was the beginning of the end for the red cars from Portello. For Ferrari it was hardly even the end of the beginning.

Hawthorn, Moss and Vanwall

In the mid 1950s British cars and drivers rose to pre-eminence in World Championship Grand Prix racing, the friendly rivalry between Stirling Moss and Mike Hawthorn capturing the public imagination in an austere post-war world. These two English stars both drove Tony Vandervell's sleek green Vanwalls, but while Hawthorn's spell with the bearing magnate's team was an unsuccessful interlude in 1955, Moss helped the team win the Constructors' Championship three years later – ironically the season in which Hawthorn took the drivers' crown at the wheel of a Ferrari.

Stirling Crauford Moss and John Michael Hawthorn were both born in 1929 and made their way into top line motor racing along distinctly different paths, although both had fathers who were closely involved with motorsport. Alfred Moss, by profession a dentist, raced at Indianapolis in 1925, while Leslie Hawthorn moved from Yorkshire to Farnham, where he bought a car repair and sales business during the 1930s, in order to be closer to Brooklands for his motorcycle racing.

Moss started racing in 1948, rising to prominence through his exploits in the closely-contested 500cc Formula 3 category, while Hawthorn started two years later driving a couple of Riley Sports cars owned by his father. Mike came to prominence in 1952 when a family friend bought him a Cooper-Bristol F2 car

and, for 1953, he was invited to drive for the Ferrari team in the second season of the World Championship run to 2-litre Formula 2 regulations.

Hawthorn scored a sensational victory in the French Grand Prix at Reims after a gripping battle with Fangio's Maserati, but World Championship F1 success would rarely come his way. In fact, his six year F1 career netted only three Grand Prix victories, the 1954 Spanish and 1958 French Grands Prix both won at the wheel of Ferraris to supplement that earlier success. Mike's bow tie and pipe became the outward trademark of a man who quickly gained a reputation for extrovert good humour and bonhomie away from the tracks, yet could be wild and unpredictable behind the wheel. And he certainly had more than his fair share of personal problems.

Unfairly pilloried in the press for dodging his national service, the truth was that Hawthorn suffered from a serious kidney ailment that would probably have prevented him from living beyond middle age. Leslie Hawthorn was killed in a road accident during 1954, so his son left Ferrari and joined Vanwall for 1955, hoping that driving for a British team would enable him to spend more time running the family business.

Sadly, he fell out with the autocratic Tony Vandervell after only three races, feeling that the four-cylinder, 2½-litre Van-

Left: Stirling Moss and Mike Hawthorn (right) chat during the 1955 Tourist Trophy meeting. Both captured the imagination of the British public although they were very different in personality.

Above right: Hawthorn's exploits with this F2 Cooper-Bristol in 1952 led to an invitation to join the factory Ferrari team for the following year.

Right: Stirling Moss at Monaco, 1955, in the Mercedes-Benz W196 in which he would later win the British Grand Prix at Aintree.

wall was not yet sufficiently developed to be a winning force. Their contract was terminated by mutual agreement, after which Hawthorn dallied again with Ferrari, but joined BRM for the 1956 season which proved similarly unsuccessful.

Moss, meanwhile, graduated to F1 via the HWM team, a determined, yet grossly underfinanced little team run by John Heath and George Abecassis from their garage, HW Motors, in Walton-on-Thames. Stirling gained enormous experience, but precious little in the way of results, and it was not until 1954, when he purchased his own Maserati 250F, that he was able to demonstrate his real skill. But for an oil leak, the brilliant young Englishman would have beaten Fangio's Mercedes to

score his first victory. As it was, it underlined his eligibility for a place in the Mercedes team and he joined Fangio behind the wheel of the straight-eight cylinder W196 for 1955.

Moss was unquestionably in a different class to Hawthorn, a natural driver as opposed to a talented artisan. Combining meticulous judgement with tremendous speed and determination, he was also extremely versatile and, when he won the 1955 British Grand Prix at Aintree by less than a length from Fangio, there would always be speculation as to whether The Old Master had slipped him the victory. Fangio later denied this, and has also been heard to remark 'Moss was the best in my time . . .'

After Mercedes withdrew at the end of 1955, Moss joined

Left: Moss in his heyday; energetic, charismatic, successful.

Below: Hawthorn won the 1954 Spanish Grand Prix in this Ferrari Super Squalo.

Right: Moss at Aintree with a Maserati 250F. He had his own such private car in 1954, then led the Italian factory team in 1956 after Mercedes pulled out of Grand Prix racing.

Maserati for whom he won the 1956 Monaco and Italian Grands Prix with the elegant works 250F, but by the end of that season he had become sufficiently impressed by the Vanwalls that he threw in his lot with Tony Vandervell for 1957.

Head of the famous bearing company, Vandervell had been among the group of industrialists administering the BRM trust when plans were laid for this national British racing car in the immediate post-war years. Before long, however, the stifling bureaucracy surrounding BRM prompted him to lay his own plans 'to beat those damned red cars', as he referred to the dominant Italian opposition.

Vandervell bought a couple of Ferraris for bearing development work during the years prior to the development of his own four-cylinder engine, the design of which was based on the concept of putting four single-cylinder Norton motorcycle engines together, operating on a common crankshaft. The Vanwall special started as 2-litre before being developed into a proper 2½-litre challenger in time for 1955 when it began to demonstrate some real promise.

At the wheel of the sleek green machines, their Colin Chapman-designed spaceframe chassis clad in elegant aerodynamic bodywork produced by Frank Costin, Moss would consolidate his reputation as the man to beat throughout the following two seasons. Moss would take over team-mate Tony Brooks' car to score Vanwall's maiden Championship triumph in the 1957 British Grand Prix at Aintree, following that up with commanding solo wins both at Pescara, and most significantly, at Monza, where he finally drove 'those damned red cars' into the ground to win the Italian Grand Prix in *una machina Inglese*.

Moss had been runner-up in the World Championship for three consecutive seasons now, but went into 1958 believing he had his best ever chance of taking the title. With Vanwall not making the trip to the first round of the title chase in Argentina, he drove Rob Walker's stubby little central-engined 2.2-litre Cooper-Climax to an historic victory which would, in due course, herald a new era in Grand Prix design technology. Then, back in Europe, he duly reeled off victories in Holland, Portugal and Morocco, yet thanks to Phil Hill dropping back behind Haw-

thorn's Ferrari Dino 246 in that final race at Casablanca, Mike emerged World Champion by the scant margin of a single point.

Vanwall had won the Constructors' Championship, totally vindicating Tony Vandervell's persistent efforts over the years, but it was a success that exacted a price which was too high. In that Moroccan Grand Prix, Moss's young team-mate Stuart Lewis-Evans crashed his Vanwall and suffered burns from which he later died, a tragedy which touched Vandervell deeply and played a large part in Vanwall's subsequent withdrawal from full-time Grand Prix racing.

The last few races of the season had seen Hawthorn driving with less than his customary enthusiasm. Since the death of his close friend and Ferrari team-mate Peter Collins in the German Grand Prix at Nurburgring, his motor racing had lost all its fun. Shortly after the last race of 1958, Hawthorn decided to hang up his helmet.

Yet he was not to live to enjoy retirement. One wet morning the following January, his Jaguar crashed, fatally injuring Britain's first World Champion driver. Moss, by contrast, still had plenty of great days ahead, although from now on he would be cast in the role of underdog, preferring to drive privately entered cars, Rob Walker's for the most part, for the three years that remained of his Grand Prix career.

From 1959 to 61 inclusive, Moss finished each season third in the World Championship, but added to his lustrous reputation by scoring Lotus's first-ever victory, at Monaco in 1960, driving Rob Walker's type 18. In the first season of the 1½-litre F1 in 1961, he produced two stunning victories, at Monaco and Nurburgring, where his four-cylinder Walker Lotus out-gunned the considerably more powerful Ferrari 156s.

Stirling's splendid record of achievement ended at Goodwood on Easter Monday 1962, when he crashed heavily in a Climax V8-engined Lotus 18/21 special during the non-Championship Glover Trophy race. It took him many months to recover from multiple injuries and, although he fully regained his health, his reactions were never restored to the high standards Stirling set himself. He chose to retire at the age of 33. Grand Prix racing had lost the man whom many still regard as the greatest of all.

Mercedes In — and Out

The 1954 French Grand Prix at Reims was an historic turning point in post-war Formula 1 history, marking as it did the return of the Mercedes-Benz team to the sport's most exalted international category. Although the Mercedes factory had been razed to the ground by allied bombing during the war, West Germany's economic resurgence during the 1950s continued at a remarkable pace and nothing symbolised that recovery more graphically than the sight of three sleek 'silver arrows' in front of the pits at the French circuit, under the militaristic management of the legendary Alfred Neubauer.

Ranged against the Ferrari 625s and Maserati 250Fs, the Mercedes-Benz W196 was an outstandingly advanced car by the standards of the day, only approached in terms of technical sophistication by the Lancia D50 V8 then under development by the financially troubled Italian company. Nestling snugly in its advanced tubular spaceframe, the engine was an in-line eight cylinder unit, angled over at 70 degrees to keep the car's lines as low as possible, with desmodromic valvegear, inboard front drum brakes and Bosch fuel injection. With a capacity of 2496cc, it developed 260bhp at 8500rpm and it was designed to be developed to around the 300bhp mark throughout its intended five year life span.

Fangio was signed to lead the driving team, although he won the Argentine Grand Prix for Maserati, being available to the Italian team until Mercedes made its debut. He would be partnered by Karl Kling and Hans Herrmann in the German line-up, but neither of these drivers could be considered in the front rank and Fangio had his work cut out as the only potential winner. In fact, time tends to throw the memory into soft-focus and the popular image of the Mercedes as all-conquering titans is far from the truth, at least as far as the 1954 season was concerned.

The all enveloping bodywork may have proved just what was needed for the wide open spaces of Reims, where Fangio and Kling scored a commanding 1-2 victory, but it certainly was not ideal at Silverstone where concrete-filled oil drums delineated

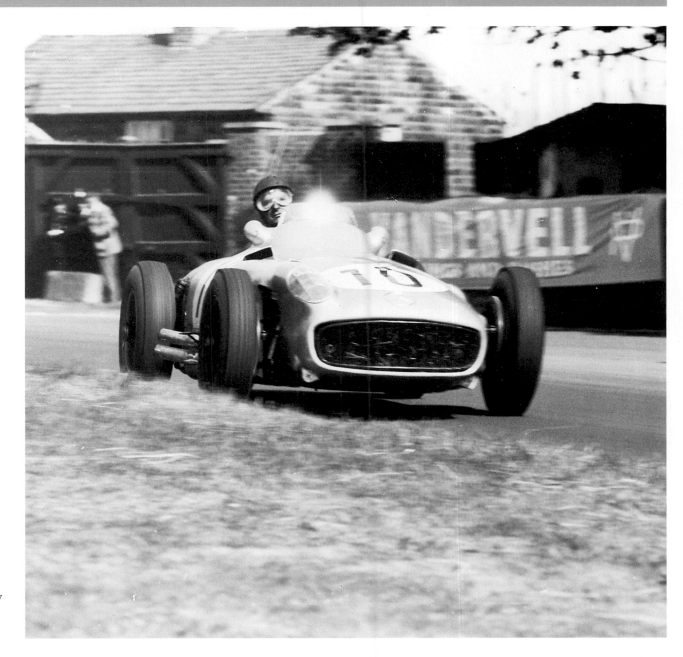

Right: Fangio in the open wheeler Mercedes W196 at Aintree in 1955, where he finished second in a 1-2-3-4 British Grand Prix grand slam led by Stirling Moss.

Below left: The all-enveloping bodywork handicapped Fangio in the 1954 British Grand Prix at Silverstone when Fangio could only finish fourth, panels badly dented by contact with the oil drum markers on the airfield circuit.

the inside of the corners. Fangio could only struggle home fourth in a race won by Froilan Gonzalez's four-cylinder Ferrari 625, a bigger-engined version of the type 500 F2 car which had dominated the Championship races throughout the previous two seasons.

For Mercedes's home race at the Nurburgring, Fangio was allotted a W196 in conventional, open-wheeler trim, and scored a commanding victory in circumstances of great personal sadness. During practice his friend and compatriot, Onofre Marimon, had crashed fatally in his Maserati and Gonzalez was so distraught that Mike Hawthorn had to take over his Ferrari 625 to finish second behind the Mercedes.

At Monza, Fangio only scraped home a lucky winner after Moss' private Maserati suffered a fractured oil pipe. Earlier in the race he had been given a very stern driving lesson by his old sparring partner Alberto Ascari who, having sat out most of the season vainly waiting for the Lancia D50 to make its race debut, was released to Ferrari for his home Grand Prix. Driving brilliantly at the wheel of a type 625 fitted with the later type 553 'Super Squalo' engine, Ascari shook himself free of Fangio to pull out a nine second lead. Only Ascari's retirement after 49 laps with a broken valve allowed Moss, and then Fangio through into first place.

Third place in Spain for Fangio at least rounded off a season in which the Argentinian driver took his second World Championship and, as far as Mercedes was concerned, 1955 could only be better with Stirling Moss eventually signing up with Fangio to form the strongest driver pairing in the business.

Fangio opened the season on a suitably optimistic note with

victory in front of his home fans in Buenos Aires, but the second round of the title chase at Monaco brought disaster. Although the team produced several permutations of chassis, with various wheelbases and the choice of either inboard or outboard brake set-ups, neither Fangio nor Moss finished and victory fell to Maurice Trintignant's plodding Ferrari 625. Ascari's Lancia D50 seemed poised to take the lead, but as Moss expired with engine problems, he inexplicably ran wide at the chicane and plunged into the harbor. A week later the great Italian champion would be killed testing a Ferrari sports car at Monza.

Thereafter, the Mercedes W196s finished first and second in the four remaining races on the Championship calendar, Fangio leading home Moss at Spa and Zandvoort, while Stirling reversed the order in front of his home crowd at Aintree to win by two-tenths of a second. Was it staged? We will probably never know, but if Fangio threw the race, he did manage it with such consumate subtlety than even Moss remains uncertain to this day.

Transmission problems accounted for Moss's retirement at Monza where Fangio led Piero Taruffi home to the final 1-2 of the season, clinching his third Championship with 40 points to Moss' 23. But the seeds of Mercedes' abrupt retirement from the sport had already been tragically sown in the Le Mans 24-hour race in June. Pierre Levegh's 300SL collided with Lance Macklin's Austin Healey, flaming debris from the wrecked German car plunging into the crowd, killing over eighty spectators.

The five year programme, and all the technical progress it promised, was prematurely abandoned. Mercedes-Benz have not been back to Formula 1 since.

The Incomparable Fangio

Juan Manuel Fangio's greatest gift was an ability to find himself in the right car at the right time, as his unmatched record of five World Championship titles certainly testifies. Throughout the fifties, up to his retirement after finishing fourth in the '58 French Grand Prix at the wheel of a Maserati, this mild mannered Argentinian was the driver by whom all others judged their progress.

Born in Balcarce, a small provincial town some 200 miles inland from Buenos Aires, Fangio was relatively old when he made his F1 debut in 1948 at the age of 37. Prior to coming to Europe to campaign a Maserati provided by the Automobile Club of Argentina, he had gained plenty of experience behind the wheel in long dusty endurance road races across the Andes in the years immediately before the Second World War. But by 1942 even in neutral Argentina the racing had come to a halt, and when it resumed in 1947, Fangio was afraid he might be too old really to make his mark.

His initial foray to Europe in '48 seemed less than totally conclusive, but an avalanche of victories followed in 1949, earning him a position with the factory Alfa Romeo team racing the classic type 158s in the first official World Championship the following season. Fangio played himself in steadily during his first season in a top team, playing a shrewd supporting role to established number one, Giuseppe Farina. But in 1951, he took his first World Championship.

The 1952 season was wiped out almost before he was able to take up his role as a member of the Maserati team. Having competed in the Ulster Trophy at Dundrod, in Northern Ireland, at the wheel of the BRM V16, he travelled by road from Paris to Monza overnight in order to drive one of the new six-cylinder Maserati A6GCMs in its first confrontation with the new Ferrari 500 in the non-title Autodrome Grand Prix.

Exhausted, he started from the back of the grid without practising, only to crash badly on the second lap, breaking a vertebra

Left: The face of the Master, Juan Manuel Fangio, World Champion 1951, 54, 55, 56 and 57.

Right: In the 1949 Gran Premio Autodrome at Monza, Fangio drove this two-stage supercharged 1½-litre Ferrari 125.

in his neck. He was invalided out for the rest of the year; indeed, his next F1 success would not come until the final race of the '53 season when he dodged through a last-corner pile-up to win the Italian Grand Prix for Maserati.

The 1954 season saw Mercedes base their Grand Prix return round his team leadership. His special blend of maturity, judgement and sheer high speed fluidity was precisely what the German team needed. Fangio displayed Latin flair with none of the temperament which so often accompanies it, so when the Mercedes W196s encountered problems, as they did on several occasions in 1954, he had the personal equilibrium to accept it. Unquestionably, his was a towering talent.

He won the Championship in 1954 and again in 1955 before Mercedes' retirement threw him into an alliance with Enzo Ferrari. He had considered retirement at the end of 1955, but the uncertain political climate within Argentina prompted him to delay that decision for at least another year. With Mercedes out, Ferrari was the only really serious option, given that Maserati was already fixed up with Moss as team leader.

For some particular reason, Fangio never felt at home in the Ferrari environment. Perhaps he felt uncomfortable joining a team he had been striving to beat for so many years, perhaps he was unsettled by the Commendatore's strategy of pitting his drivers against each other in an unspoken psychological battle to see which would assert himself as team leader. He was partnered by Luigi Musso, Eugenio Castellotti and Peter Collins, the team now using further uprated versions of the Lancia D50 which Maranello had inherited (and some would say technically vandalised) when the rival Italian car company collapsed the previous year.

Helped by team-mate Peter Collins, who relinquished his car to Fangio both at Spa and Monaco, the Argentinian took his fourth World Championship title in surroundings which felt less than totally hospitable. But for his generosity, the young driver from Kidderminster would almost certainly have become England's first World Champion driver two years ahead of his close pal Mike Hawthorn.

In 1957, Fangio returned to the Maserati fold for his final complete World Championship season, battling against the resur-

Right: Fangio's Maserati 250F leads Stirling Moss' Vanwall in the 1958 French Grand Prix, the Argentinian's last race. He finished fourth.

Below: Fangio is seen here at Silverstone in 1953, trying his hand with the fearsome BRM V16. His relationship with the British team was fleeting and unsuccessful.

gent Vanwalls as his most prominent opposition. From the start of the season, he reeled off the victories; Buenos Aires, Monaco, Rouen-les-Essarts, before coming up against engine failure at Aintree which cleared the way for the Moss/Brooks Vanwall victory.

On 4 August 1957, Fangio scored what was to be his last Grand Prix victory, and almost certainly his greatest. While Ferrari's trio of V8 Lancia-engined Tipo 801s of Hawthorn, Collins and Luigi Musso were scheduled to run non-stop through the 22 lap race round the challenging 14-mile Nurburgring, the Maserati 150F seemed to have a tyre wear problem that would require Fangio to stop.

Accordingly, the World Champion attempted to turn this handicap to his advantage, opting to start with a light fuel load. Starting from pole position, he initially held back while he played himself in, but as the already-minimal fuel load lightened, he confidently surged into the lead on lap three. In a sensational display of virtuoso driving, he pulled away at an amazing seven seconds a lap, only to have his advantage negated by a shambolic 53-second tyre change and refuelling stop at the end of lap 12. By the time he resumed the chase in third place, he was over 45 seconds behind Hawthorn and Collins.

It took a couple of laps for the Great Man to get back in his stride once again, but then the Ferraris' advantage began to crumble as the Maserati team leader piled on the pressure. Shattering the lap record repeatedly, the gap was 33 seconds on

lap 15, 25.5s on lap 17 and 13.5s by lap 19. On lap twenty, Hawthorn, Collins and Fangio stormed past the pits, the two Ferraris and one Maserati covered by just two seconds.

Fangio cut inside Collins to take second place going into the North Curve and finally forced ahead of Hawthorn to take the lead on the tricky downhill approach to the Adenau bridge. He went into the last lap leading Hawthorn by three seconds, eventually winning by just over four.

This success represented the final World Championship Grand Prix triumph for that elegant machine, the six-cylinder 2493cc Maserati 250F which, to hosts of admirers, was the embodiment of the classic, front-engined 2½-litre Formula 1 car. Fangio had scored its very first Grand Prix victory in Buenos Aires at the start of the 1954 season and now rounded off its front-line career on the highest possible note. Perhaps surprisingly, in view of the historical status attaching to the car, the 250F won a mere seven World Championship Grands Prix only in the hands of Fangio and Stirling Moss. Yet it also achieved considerable success in non-championship events and was the ultimate private entrants' machine of its era.

In the middle of the following season, Fangio would retire having won 24 of the 51 Grands Prix in which he competed, having started from pole position on 28 occasions. In old age, he continued to radiate a serene dignity and power which could be quite awesome. Truly, Juan Manuel Fangio was one of the most dynamic performers the sport has ever known.

Cooper's Quiet Revolution

Charles Cooper and his son John began the decade building spindly little 500cc Formula 3 cars, from which enormously successful base, they would end the 1950s initiating the central-engined Grand Prix design revolution which would change the face of Formula 1 for all time.

They built their first single seater, based round chassis components from a couple of Fiat Topolino saloons, powered by a JAP single cylinder engine, in 1946 and were in at the ground floor as the 500cc F3 took off as a training ground for future Grand Prix talent. Stirling Moss and Peter Collins, who would mature into two of Britain's F1 winners in the 1950s, served their apprenticeship in this frantic, action-packed formula where Coopers proliferated.

The father and son Cooper partnership was uniquely balanced, John's sometimes over-ambitious, effervescent enthusiasm tempered by the Old Man's fundamental conservatism and reluctance to spend money unless it was absolutely necessary. From a small factory in Surbiton, near London, the Cooper Car Company rose to its absolute zenith of achievement in 1959 and 60, but had withered and vanished from the scene completely by the end of the following decade.

Cooper applied the principle of its central-engined, Coventry Climax FWA-engined 'Bob Tail' sports cars to the construction of an F1 'special' with all enveloping bodywork and propelled by a 2.2-litre Bristol six-cylinder engine. They were persuaded to pursue this course of development by gritty Australian rising star Jack Brabham who had arrived on the British scene at the end of 1954 after achieving considerable success in his native land at the wheel of a front-engined Cooper-Bristol F2 machine. Brabham drove this Cooper special in the British Grand Prix at Aintree, marking the constructor's F1 debut, although it was a low-key affair and he retired from the race with an overheating engine.

From the start of 1957 Cooper really got into the swing of things, pitching his F2 Climax-engined machinery into the battle for Grand Prix supremacy and proving that a modestly powered, light and agile central-engined car could do effective battle with the established 2½-litre front-engined runners. Their best placing in a Championship event came when Roy Salvadori's 2-litre works T43 finished fifth in the British Grand Prix at Silverstone, but 1958 was to see the crucial breakthrough with the first Cooper victory.

Left: John Cooper in his early 500cc prototype single seater at the Prescott hill climb in 1949.

Above: Stirling Moss cut his racing teeth on a Cooper-Norton in the 500cc Formula 3 which was Britain's domestic single seater nursery through much of the following decade.

Right: Jochen Rindt in the V12 Maserati-engined Cooper T81 in the 1966 French Grand Prix at Reims.

Left: John Cooper out testing again, this time in one of the early rear-engined Formula 2 cars.

Below: Formula 1 success as Jack Brabham heads his Climax four-cylinder Formula 1 type T53 to victory in the 1960 Belgian Grand Prix at Spa-Francorchamps.

At the start of 1958, the 2½-litre F1 was extended for another three seasons, although the Commission Sportif Internationale (CSI – as the governing body was then known) changed the fuel regulations, prohibiting the use of methanol fuels and requiring the use of AvGas aviation spirit, a 100-130 octane fuel which was far more economical. In addition, race distances were cut from a 500km minimum to 300km. The new season was scheduled to start at Monaco in May, but the Automobile Club of Argentina applied to run a race on 19 January. Vanwall and BRM were unready, so Stirling Moss was released to drive a 2-litre Cooper for Rob Walker.

Starting seventh on the ten car grid, Moss was able to put the Maserati and Ferrari opposition under intense pressure from the start, the bigger front-engined cars ponderous and less agile with a heavy fuel load. By lap 35 of the 80 lap race he had inherited the lead when Fangio's Maserati stopped for fresh tyres. Stirling was extremely concerned about conserving his own rubber, knowing that the four-bolt fixing on the Cooper wheels would destroy his chances if he had to stop. But it all went to plan and Moss successfully duped the opposition, running through non-stop to win from Luigi Musso's Ferrari, despite a vain, late-race challenge from the Italian when he woke up to the fact that the Cooper was not going to make the expected pit stop after all.

Rob Walker's Cooper would win again in 1958, French journeyman Maurice Trintignant triumphing at Monaco after the faster opposition retired. Salvadori and Trintignant would later finish second and third in the German Grand Prix, another portent of what was to come in 1959.

By now Jack Brabham had become an absolutely central component in the Cooper team's Grand Prix efforts. The taciturn Aussie was a born mechanic, prepared to work all hours to help prepare the team's cars, and got on particularly well with John Cooper. His rugged, head-down, opposite-lock style at the wheel of the four-cylinder Climax-engined Cooper would become a trademark over the next two seasons as the team from Surbiton rose to humble the front-engined Ferrari Dino 246s and BRM

P25s which would represent their prime opposition through to the end of the 2½-litre formula.

Through 1959, Brabham would be partnered by young New Zealander Bruce McLaren and the bespectacled Masten Gregory from Kansas City. Brabham would win at Monaco and Aintree, Stirling Moss in the Walker car at Lisbon and Monza, while young McLaren rounded off the season victorious in the US Grand Prix at Sebring, where an exhausted Brabham pushed his out-of-fuel T51 home fourth to clinch the Championship in a dramatic fashion.

Appreciating that Colin Chapman's new Lotus 18 would be a tough nut to crack, Cooper's designer Owen Maddock produced the more compact T53 'Lowline' for Brabham and McLaren to use through 1960. It proved to be absolutely the right car at the right moment. In Jack's hands it reeled off victories at Zandvoort, Spa, Reims, Silverstone and Oporto to put the Australian driver's second successive title beyond doubt. Not until Alain Prost's Championships of 1985 and 86 would another driver retain the crown.

From then onwards, Cooper's star faded gently. The onset of the 1½-litre F1 meant that the Surbiton team was no longer using its central-engined concept to outclass the front-engined dinosaurs. From now on, Grand Prix cars would be smaller, lighter, more compactly engineered. Lotus certainly, and even BRM and Ferrari, would gradually eclipse Cooper in this respect. In 1962, Brabham went off to form his own F1 team, and McLaren's '62 Monaco triumph would be the marque's sole F1 win in the years up to 1965.

In 1964, Charles Cooper died at the age of 71. Son John, still recuperating from the after-effects of a serious road accident the previous year, was left feeling uneasy and rather uncertain about the future. He sold the company to the Chipstead Group, the British Maserati importers controlled by Mario Tozzi-Condivi and Jonathan Sieff, grandson of Marks and Spencer driving force Lord Sieff. John stayed involved in running the F1 team, but a considerable administrative burden had been removed from his shoulders.

Into the 3-litre F1 at the start of 1966, the newly backed Cooper team did a deal to use uprated 3-litre versions of the old 60-degree V12 originally built for the Maserati 250F almost a decade earlier. The Cooper T81-Maserati was a lumpy, technically unsophisticated beast, but was adequately competitive, particularly in the hands of Jochen Rindt and Ferrari refugee John Surtees, the latter wiping his former employers in the eye by taking the Anglo-Italian hybrid to victory in the Mexican Grand Prix.

New boy Pedro Rodriguez scored a lucky victory at the start of 1967 in South Africa, but F1 was soon entering the era of Cosworth's new DFV V8 and Cooper's technology just was not in a position to keep up. Losing a financially crucial Firestone contract at the start of 1968 marked the beginning of the end. Although the team fielded the elegant new T86B, powered by BRM's latest V12, in 1968, driven variously by Brian Redman, Lodovico Scarfiotti, Lucien Bianchi and rally man Vic Elford, the team had been left behind, both technically and financially. It closed its doors for good at the end of the season.

Part 3

The 1960s

Ferrari Quick Off the Mark

On 29 October 1958, an announcement was made within the hallowed portals of the Royal Automobile Club in London's Pall Mall which would shake the British Formula 1 fraternity to its core. At a reception held to present awards to Mike Hawthorn and Tony Vandervell, recognising their success in the World Championship for Drivers and Constructors respectively, CSI President Auguste Perouse stunned everybody into silence with the news that a new 1½-litre F1, with a 500kg minimum weight limit, would supersede the current 2½-litre F1 from the start of the 1961 season.

The British were absolutely outraged at the way in which the sport's governing body had adopted a proposal put forward by France, a country which had nothing to offer in the way of racing cars, for this planned new formula. Ironically, although only Britain and Italy came out in favour of retaining the 2½-litre limit, it was the latter's most famous team which would grasp the technical initiative and virtually sweep the board when the 1961 season finally got underway.

While British constructors wasted a lot of time producing plans for the 3-litre 'Intercontinental Formula', which turned out to be nothing more than a domestic formule libre series, Ferrari pressed on with its 1½-litre engine development programme. Throughout the final three years of the 2½-litre F1, the Italian team had continued developing a small capacity version of its 65-degree V6 engine for F2 purposes and it was this unit that formed the basis of the 1961 challenge.

At the end of the 1960 season, Ferrari's chief engineer Carlo Chiti produced a 120-degree version of the V6 engine which developed around 190bhp at 9500rpm, a figure more than adequate to deal with the makeweight four cylinder Coventry Climax engines used by the vast majority of the British opposition. Both Climax and BRM were working flat-out on their own V8 designs, but these would not see the light of day until midway

Above: Enzo Ferrari; smiling with the confidence of a winner.

Right: Stripped naked, the 1961 Ferrari 156, this example fitted with the earlier 65-degree V6 engine.

Left: Phil Hill heading for victory in the Italian Grand Prix to clinch the 1961 World Championship.

Previous page: Start of an epic battle as Jochen Rindt's Lotus 49C and Jackie Stewart's Matra MS10 rocket away from the Silverstone grid as the 1969 British Grand Prix gets underway.

through the '61 season, by which time the battle had already been lost.

The Ferrari V6 engines were installed in spaceframe chassis clothed in distinctive bodywork, a feature of which was the twin nostril 'shark's nose' treatment of the front end. Drive was by means of a five-speed transaxle mounted inboard of the rear axle line, thereby allowing sufficient space in the engine bay for a possible 2.9-litre engine to be installed should the Intercontinental formula get off the ground. Ferrari had a well-honed reputation for hedgeing his bets!

The driver line-up included Americans Phil Hill and Richie Ginther, both products of the US West Coast domestic racing scene, and the aristocratic German Count Wolfgang von Trips. Later in the year they would be joined by the brilliantly talented 19-year old Mexican Ricardo Rodriguez, while Italian novice Giancarlo Baghetti, running under the auspices of a group of Italian racing teams, was fielded as part of a plan to foster home-grown driving talent.

It was Baghetti, driving in his first F1 race, who gave the Ferrari 156 its victorious race debut at the non-championship Syracuse Grand Prix in Sicily, but when it came to the first round of the World Championship at Monaco there was a very different outcome waiting. At the wheel of Rob Walker's private Lotus 18, with its four-cylinder Climax engine, Stirling Moss drove with typical brilliance to win from Ginther's Ferrari by just over three seconds.

That same afternoon, Baghetti was busy winning his second non-title race at Naples, while the second event on the Championship calendar saw von Trips leading from start to finish in the Dutch Grand Prix at Zandvoort. At Spa, for the Belgian Grand Prix, Maranello followed that up with a stupendous 1-2-3-4 finish in the order Hill, von Trips and Ginther with Belgian sports car hero Olivier Gendebien completing the grand slam.

Despite establishing this level of domination, the Ferrari team did not provide a desperately happy or secure working environment for its drivers during 1961. Enzo Ferrari kept his employees on their toes by consistently declining to nominate a team leader, with the result that time-wasting internecine battles very nearly jeopardised the outcome of several races. The tension built up particularly between Hill and von Trips, although Ginther let it all pass him by, having a rather more philosophical approach to his chosen sport.

Baghetti was included in the team for the French Grand Prix at Reims, which was just as well as things turned out. With Hill, Ginther and von Trips all retiring, Maranello's honour was left solely in the hands of this new boy. Driving the old 65-degree engined car with considerable flair and control in simply torrid conditions, he held off Dan Gurney's four-cylinder Porsche to become the only driver so far in the sport's history to win his very first Grand Prix.

The British Grand Prix at Aintree also took place in traditionally English summer weather. Von Trips drove brilliantly

Left: Ferrari's sleek 'shark nose' type 156s line up in front of the pits in preparation for the '61 Belgian Grand Prix at Spa-Francorchamps.

Above: Richie Ginther finished fifth in the 1961 Dutch Grand Prix at Zandvoort, a race won by his teammate Wolfgang von Trips (*above right*).

Right: Giancarlo Baghetti's semi-works Ferrari 156 battles with Dan Gurney's Porsche for the lead of the 1961 French Grand Prix at Reims. Baghetti came out ahead by a matter of feet, thereby becoming the only driver in F1 history to have won a World Championship Grand Prix at his first attempt.

Left: Richie Ginther's Ferrari 156 chased Stirling Moss all the way to finish a close second in the 1961 Monaco Grand Prix.

Below: Wolfgang von Trips was poised to take the 1961 World Championship when he was killed in a second lap collision with Jim Clark's Lotus during the Italian Grand Prix at Monza.

Right: Jim Clark at the wheel of the monocoque Lotus 25 during its race debut in the 1962 Dutch Grand Prix at Zandvoort.

Below right: Clark, in the cockpit, and design genius Colin Chapman discuss the merits of the trend-setting Lotus 25.

to win in torrential rain, but similar conditions at the 14-mile Nurburgring saw Stirling Moss weave his magic yet again and pull off a repeat of his Monaco success in the Walker team Lotus 18. Von Trips and Hill were second and third, so the outcome of the World Championship hung in the balance between the two Ferrari team mates as they went into the psychologically demanding Italian Grand Prix at Monza.

This was the race at which young Ricardo Rodriguez made his debut, unbelievably qualifying on the front row of the grid a mere one-tenth of a second slower than von Trips. Clearly this young Mexican had a great deal of promise, but it was not for Rodriguez's display of dauntless flair that this race would go down in the history books. Instead, that September Sunday marked one of the most tragic episodes in post-war motor racing when von Trips tangled with Jim Clark's Lotus 21 coming up to complete the second lap of the race. The wayward Ferrari bounced down the spectactor fence, killing fourteen members of the public, and the popular German driver also succumbed to his injuries.

Three of the four remaining Ferraris gradually dropped out with mechanical problems, leaving Phil Hill to take the chequered flag and clinch the World Championship. But it was an uncomfortable moment for this serious, cultured and sensitive Californian and any euphoria was dampened considerably in the wake of the dreadful tragedy which had befallen von Trips.

The Ferrari team missed the United States Grand Prix at Watkins Glen, an understandable disappointment for the new World Champion. He would stay on with the World Champion team for 1962, but such loyalty effectively marked the end of his career. Maranello fell from the technical high wire, overwhelmed by the surging tide of British V8s which would completely eclipse Ferrari's efforts. Within another 12 months, it would seem that the 1961 domination was nothing but a dream.

The Days of Jimmy Clark

Jim Clark, who died at the age of 32 when his Formula 2 Lotus 48 crashed at Hockenheim on 7 April 1968 is recalled affectionately by his many fans as the greatest driver the world has ever known.

Fellow Scot Jackie Stewart knows all the arguments in favour of one driver or another, but has also come out as a supporter of the theory that Clark was, quite simply, The Best. This verdict comes from a man who not only raced against him regularly in F1 from 1965 through to the first race of 1968, shortly before Jim's death, but himself won three World Championship titles to Clark's two. Stewart's verdict underlines the reality that Championships alone form an incomplete index of a Grand Prix driver's talent.

Younger readers may find it difficult to understand the feelings of disbelief which surged through motor racing that Monday morning in 1968. We now live in an age where every Grand Prix driver believes himself to be the best and can offer one hundred and one reasons why he is not winning every race. But in the mid 1960s, Clark was held in awe by most of his top-line rivals. Assuming he had a halfway decent car, his superiority guaranteed that the others would be racing for second place.

But what sort of a person was Jim Clark? Over the years many words have been written about him and about his career, yet

here I am attempting to add to this mountain of copy a few weeks after the 21st anniversary of his death.

The quality that made Jim Clark so very different was the fact that he did not pursue success with enormous zeal. To say it came by accident might be to over-exaggerate the situation, but the truth of the matter is that he only tried his hand in racing, back in Scotland in the late 1950s, purely out of interest in discovering what the feeling was like cut on a racing circuit at the wheel of a car.

Speaking of his very first race, at the bleak, wind-swept Crimond circuit, near Perth, Clark said; 'I think at that point I was driven by the sheer curiosity of seeing what it was actually like out there on a race track rather than a burning desire to beat everybody.'

'This curiosity has stayed with me and was partly responsible for me going to Indianapolis in 1963 because I was fascinated to see what was said to be "the capital of auto racing" although I didn't agree with that assessment and found it all a bit brash and pretentious!'

Clark's racing apprenticeship was served out against a background of considerable parental concern. His father had wanted him to concentrate on farming at the family farm, Edington Mains, nestling in the Scottish border country near the sleepy village of Chirnside. But Jim had a firm and growing resolution that he was going to make motor racing his life, come what may, and even tried to justify it to his father by telling him that he believed this was a hobby he could make pay for itself!

'I suppose, in a way, if I had set out to be a Grand Prix driver and made it my life's ambition, then I might have felt a greater sense of achievement. But, really, I tried to fight against it to a certain extent.'

The image of this reticent young man stumbling on the 1963 World Championship almost by accident may seem a trifle far-

fetched, but that is almost the way it was. His brilliant talent at club racing level was recognised and nurtured by the late, great Colin Chapman and, of course, their racing record together during the early 1960s is now a matter of legend.

Driving the superb Chapman-designed Lotus-Climax 1½-litre Grand Prix contenders, Clark held GP racing in a vice-like grip between 1962 and 65. Then came the switch to the 3-litre F1 and by the summer of 1967, the Cosworth DFV-engined Lotus 49 was available to Jim. Again, he was the pace-setter, the front runner par excellence. He was the man by whom all others judged their progress.

His first Championship victory was at the wheel of a Lotus 24 in the 1962 Belgian Grand Prix at Spa, an event he would also win for the following three consecutive years. His last came barely six years later, in South Africa, with the Cosworth-engined Lotus 49. It was supremely appropriate that this final triumph should be victory number 25, eclipsing Juan Manuel Fangio's previous record of 24 victories.

The history books may show that he only won two world titles, in 1963 and 65, but he missed taking the '62 and '64 championships by a hair's breadth and the truth of the matter is that he dominated the Grand Prix scene throughout his career. When Jim had a good car, the battle was for second place. He and Chapman also stormed the most sacred bastion of American oval racing, winning the Indianapolis 500 on their third attempt in 1965 and ending the age of the front-engined roadsters which had previously dominated at the Brickyard.

However, the satisfaction he derived from it all was intensely personal and individualistic. 'It's not so much the racing, more the satisfaction of driving a car on the absolute limit and still

being in control of it. That's the greatest feeling of fascination that I get from this business.'

Yet what made him such a hero? Truth be told, he was just such a shy, ordinary man. He was very private, too, loving his close friends from his home village and still privately nurturing the feeling that he might one day return to the Scottish borders and continue farming. Jackie Stewart, however, believes that to be an unrealistic view. 'By the end of his life he was becoming much more sophisticated and worldly-wise,' says Jackie. 'I honestly don't think he would have returned to the business of farming . . .'

Shy, quiet and with an in-bred sense of what was right and what was wrong, Jim Clark was an unlikely hero. The man with the quiet, lilting Scottish accent and quiet manner would bite his finger-nails down to the quick in an outward display of nervousness when he was away from the cockpit.

But, at the wheel of a Grand Prix car, he was an artist; cool, competitive and utterly uncompromising. There are people in Britain today, like the author, who never talked to him, yet regarded him as a friend.

That is what made Jim Clark so very special.

Left: Clark's Lotus 25, with its distinctive yellow painted wheels, lines up on pole position for the 1963 British Grand Prix at Silverstone flanked by Dan Gurney's Brabham and Graham Hill's BRM. On the second row are John Surtees' Ferrari and the Coopers of Bruce McLaren and Tony Maggs.

Below left: Jim Clark, that gentle genius.

Above right: Clark leads team-mate Graham Hill in their Lotus 49s during the 1967 French Grand Prix held on the Le Mans Bugatti circuit.

Right: Clark leads Jackie Stewart's Matra and Jochen Rindt's Brabham-Repco on the opening lap of the 1968 South African Grand Prix, the last win of his F1 career in which he topped Fangio's record of 24 victories.

Brabham Keeps it Simple

It was absolutely characteristic of the pragmatic Jack Brabham that he should seek out the most practical, available and straightforward solution to solve his team's pressing engine requirements for the 3-litre Formula 1 which came into force at the start of 1966.

The Repco company had been established in Australia before the Second World War as Replacement Parts Pty., a commercial supplier of replacement components for road cars. By the early 1960s, it had grown into an enormously successful business, exporting from Australia to 85 other countries and expanding into many other areas of specialist engineering.

Repco had some room available at its English premises in Surbiton, Surrey, and when Brabham's fledgling company, Motor Racing Developments, began manufacturing production cars for the junior formulae in England, it rented some of that floor space. This led to a minor sponsorship arrangement which saw all the Brabham cars built for the junior formulae labelled as 'Repco Brabhams'. It was to prove the start of a fortuitous partnership.

While Brabham was busy contesting the remaining years of the 1½-litre Formula 1 with his Coventry-Climax V-8-engined cars, Repco became involved in building a new racing engine. This was intended to replace the long-lived, four cylinder Coventry-Climax FPF unit which had for many years provided the life blood in the Tasman formula, Australasia's premier single seater racing category.

Repco engineers Frank Hallam and Phil Irving produced a new V8 based round the General Motors Oldsmobile F85 linerless aluminium cylinder block, a project which had been shelved by GM after it abandoned plans for a 3½-litre Buick 'compact' sedan on the US market.

The Repco V8 spluttered into life as a 2.5-litre Tasman engine in the spring of 1965, but Jack Brabham had by now realised the possibilities it offered and applied all his powers of persuasion to tempt Repco into committing to a full-blown Grand Prix programme for 1966. The decision was eventually made in favour of such a step and the first Brabham-Repco raced in the non-Championship South African Grand Prix at East London on New Year's Day, 1966. Jack would have won easily had the debutant V8 not seized its injection pump while well in command.

Left: The Oldsmobile V8-derived Repco engine powered Jack Brabham and Denny Hulme to the World Championship in 1966 and 67 respectively.

Above right: Jack Brabham had won two World Championships for Cooper in 1959 and 60 before adding a third to his tally, with a car bearing his own name, in 1966.

Right: Jack's Brabham heading for victory in the 1966 Silverstone International Trophy race at the start of a Championship-winning season.

BRABHAM KEEPS IT SIMPLE

At the start of the new Formula 1, most teams were in a state of technical disarray. The Cooper-Maserati alliance attempted to get by with uprated versions of an outdated V12 engine from the 1950s. BRM was bogged down with its over-complex H-16 which Lotus also hoped to use as a stop-gap measure. Only Ferrari, as usual, seemed organised from the outset and the Italian team's new V12-engined car in the hands of John Surtees seemed likely favourite for the Championship.

However, the form book was dramatically overturned when Jack's new Brabham-Repco, with its lightweight and simple spaceframe chassis and compact V8 engine, out-ran Surtees to win the non-championship Silverstone International Trophy, a pre-season 'taster' which traditionally provided a useful pointer to what might follow when the title chase got underway. Sure enough, although out of luck at Monaco and Spa, Brabham became the first man to win a Grand Prix in a car bearing his own name when he triumphed in the French Grand Prix at Reims on 3 July.

By this time Surtees had fallen out with Ferrari and had stormed off to join the Cooper-Maserati combine, effectively making life a lot easier for Brabham as he picked off victories in the British, Dutch and German Grands Prix throughout the summer. As the season progressed, taciturn New Zealander Denny Hulme grew in stature as Brabham's number two and was clearly aiming for his own first Grand Prix victory, although as events turned out he would have to wait until 1967 to realise that ambition.

Brabham clinched his third World Championship, adding to those scored with Cooper in 1959 and 60, at the 1966 Italian

Grand Prix even though he failed to finish. But Jack knew only too well that his team's success had been achieved largely through the weakness of the opposition. In 1967 Repco strengthened its challenge by building a revised version of the V8, dubbed the type 740, round their own purpose-built cylinder block.

However, things would not be so easy for the Brabham-Repcos in 1967. Although the new engines would produce in the region of 330bhp at 8000rpm, this was not going to be sufficient to deal with the new Ford-financed Cosworth V8 engine which was under development for Team Lotus. By the time Jim Clark gave the Lotus 49 its maiden victory at Zandvoort it was fairly clear that Cosworth had squeezed 390bhp out of this sensational new engine. But although Clark would win four Grands Prix that season, the Brabham-Repcos had been steadily gathering points from the word go, this time Denny Hulme pipping Brabham to the Championship on the strength of two wins (Monaco and Germany) and a succession of consistent placings. Hulme finished on 51 points, five ahead of Brabham.

For 1968, Repco attempted to compete with Cosworth by developing an ambitious four-cam V8, the type 860, but although it hovered around the 400bhp mark when it was running, the latest version of the Australian engine proved horrifyingly unreliable. With Hulme switching to McLaren, Brabham was now partnered by the mercurial Jochen Rindt, but even his genius could only produce a single third place at the Nurburgring. A similar placing in South Africa at the start of the year had been achieved by Rindt driving the team's 1967 machine.

By the end of 1968 it was clear that the Brabham-Repco partnership had run its course. Attempting to operate along a 12,000 mile supply route from Repco's base near Melbourne to Brabham's racing base in Surrey had become just too technically wearing. Unable to fight against the prevailing tide, in 1969 Jack's team switched to using the more reliable Cosworth V8, which, unlike the Repco, could be installed in the chassis as a stressed member. A World Championship-winning partnership was at an end.

BRABHAM KEEPS IT SIMPLE

Above left: Denny Hulme on his way to victory in the 1967 Monaco Grand Prix.

Far left: The four-cam version of the Repco V8 proved very unreliable throughout 1968.

Left: Jack on his way to victory in the 1960 French Grand Prix at Reims for Cooper. Six years later, on the same circuit, he would score his first Grand Prix victory in a car bearing his own name.

Above: Jack en route to victory in the 1966 British Grand Prix at Brands Hatch.

Right: Denny Hulme was a tough campaigner and battled hard with his employer to win the 1967 Championship.

BRM Peaks and Fades

British Racing Motors was established in 1945 with a view to manufacturing a British national Grand Prix car which would benefit from the financial and technical support of the entire motor industry rather than being supported by a single wealthy patron. The men behind the concept were Raymond Mays and Peter Berthon, both of whom had been extensively involved in the international motor racing scene since the post World War I years, Mays forging a considerable reputation for his driving exploits at the wheel of an ERA, the company behind which they fulfilled pivotal founding roles. ERA had operated from premises within the grounds of Eastgate House, the Mays family home at Bourne, Lincolnshire, and BRM would also make the small provincial town its life-long base.

BRM's first project was the 1½-litre supercharged V16 Formula 1 contender which, late off the mark and beset with technical problems, raced only spasmodically in the formula for which it was designed. By the time its complex and very powerful engine was massaged into some semblance of reliability, such was the dearth of competitive cars that the 1952 and 53 World Championship regulations had been changed to cater solely for Formula 2 machines. Thus the original BRM eked out a twilight existence with what were intended to be morale-boosting outings in British domestic events.

Far from benefitting by the publicity attaching to its cause, those motor industry backers who had supported the BRM project now found themselves strongly criticised for its continuing failure. The original project foundered amid considerable bad

feeling, but BRM was bought by the Owen Organisation, one of the country's largest privately owned industrial empires, later to become part of GKN. The head of this empire was Mr – later Sir – Alfred Owen, a serious-minded Methodist with an enormous enthusiasm for the sport backed up by a shrewd business mind.

With the onset of the 2½-litre F1 at the start of 1955, BRM produced one of its most attractive machines, the four-cylinder type P25 designed by Stuart Tresilian. However, it was not until 1959 that the team won its first Grand Prix, Swedish driver Jo Bonnier triumphing in the Dutch Grand Prix at Zandvoort.

The development of a compact 60-degree V8 engine for the new 1½-litre F1 and a major organisational shake-up at the start of 1962 brought about increased responsibility and influence for talented former Rolls-Royce engineer Tony Rudd. With Graham Hill and American Richie Ginther forming a strong driving partnership, BRM looked set for its best season in 1962. It certainly needed it, for Alfred Owen decreed that, unless the team won two Grands Prix during the course of the year, it faced closure.

After Hill reeled off the first win in the Dutch Grand Prix, Rudd wrote to Mr. Owen optimistically speculating about plans for 1963. But Rudd was running ahead of events; back came a reply from the company's patriarch reminding him that BRM had to win two races if its future was to be secured. But Rudd need not have worried. Hill scored another superb victory in the rain-soaked German Grand Prix and all was well.

Left: BRM's 1½-litre V8 won the team its sole World Championship in 1962.

Above right: Graham Hill was BRM's stalwart from 1960 to 66, seen here in the 64 Belgian Grand Prix with the 1½-litre V8-engined car.

Right: Richie Ginther's BRM leads Dan Gurney's Porsche during the 1962 British Grand Prix at Aintree.

Left: Graham Hill leads Jackie Stewart in the 1965 Italian Grand Prix at Monza. Their V8 BRMs finished second and first respectively.

Below left: Stewart with the 2-litre 'Tasman' V8 during the 1966 Dutch Grand Prix. These enlarged 1½-litre cars were used while the team tried to sort out the H-16 during the first year of the 3-litre Formula 1.

Right: Graham Hill tries the BRM H-16 during practice for the 1966 French Grand Prix at Reims.

Below: The H-16 engine proved quite a challenge to package neatly in the BRM chassis.

Battling against Jimmy Clark's new monocoque Lotus 25, Hill was in contention for the World Championship all the way to the final race, the South African Grand Prix at East London on New Year's Eve. Whichever of them won would be Champion, but while Clark set the pace from the start, his retirement due to an oil leak handed the race – and title – to Graham Hill.

The moustachioed Londoner would become synonymous with BRM over the next few years, winning a hat trick of Monaco victories from 1963-65 and coming tantalisingly close to taking another Championship for the Bourne team in 1964, only to see it snatched by the Ferrari-mounted John Surtees in the very last race.

The little BRM V8 was an absolute jewel, winning the 1965

Tasman Championship in 2-litre guise and powering the team to second place in the Championship each year from 1963 to 65. These were BRM's golden days when this highly competent team amply rewarded the faith invested in it by the Owen Organisation. However, with the onset of the 3-litre F1 in 1966, Tony Rudd presided over what was later seen to be a vital technical stumble.

Understandably encouraged by the outstanding success of the V8, Rudd effectively 'flattened out' the V8 engine to 180-degrees and then harnessed two such engines together, their two crankshafts geared together. Thus the complex BRM H-16 engine came into existence, Rudd confidently predicting it would produce somewhere in the region of 600bhp once fully developed.

Unfortunately, not only was the new engine beset by massive vibration problems which literally threatened to shake it apart on the test bed, it barely produced 400bhp. It was supremely ironic that the only race victory scored by the H-16 BRM engine was achieved by Jim Clark when it was installed in a Lotus 43. The Scot won the 1966 United States Grand Prix, using a spare works engine borrowed from BRM and installed in the car the night before the race!

Colin Chapman certainly knew what he was doing using the H-16 only as an interim power unit while the new Cosworth V8 was under development. But BRM struggled on with the H-16 through 1967, Jackie Stewart and Mike Spence finishing second and fifth in the Belgian Grand Prix to record the works team's best result with that complex engine.

The H-16 was shelved at the end of 1967 after which a brand new V12 replaced it for the following year. With Mike Spence now joined by Pedro Rodriguez in the wake of Stewart's departure to join the newly established Tyrrell outfit, the Bourne

team radiated a fresh mood of optimism seemingly justified by both drivers' performance in the early season British domestic non-championship races. But then it suffered a major body blow when Spence was killed testing a Lotus turbine car at Indianapolis. The young driver from Maidenhead had been an important motivating force and the team's momentum was gradually dissipated over the balance of the year.

For 1969, John Surtees was recruited to drive for the team and great hopes were pinned on the new BRM P139 for which a further revised version of the V12 engine was prepared. Sadly, the team's fortunes plummetted to fresh depths of dejection, only a third place at Watkins Glen alleviating the despair. Added to this, Sir Alfred Owen suffered a serious stroke which rendered him almost totally incapacitated through to his death in 1974, so in some ways the real story of BRM ended with the decade.

Top left: John Surtees struggles to keep the BRM P139 ahead of Bruce McLaren during the 1969 Spanish Grand Prix.

Left: Jean-Pierre Beltoise scored BRM's last victory, at Monaco in 1972.

Below: Five BRM P160s contested the 1971 Canadian Grand Prix. They were driven by George Eaton, Helmut Marko, Peter Gethin, Howden Ganley and Jo Siffert.

Right: Jean-Pierre Beltoise at the Nurburgring, 1966, with a Formula 2 Matra.

Below right: A 1968 F1 Matra being worked on at the Tyrrell team's Ockham headquarters.

The French Connection

France has a well-established history in the roots of motor racing, but when the Gordini team finally laid down its arms and retired from Grand Prix racing in 1956, eleven years would elapse before that proud country would be stirred into Formula 1 action once more. In April 1967 Georges Pompidou's government made a grant of six million francs (then worth about £800,000/$2,000,000) to the Matra-Sport organisation for the development of a car which would put France back on the Grand Prix map.

Matra-Sport had been established in October 1964 as a motor racing subsidiary of the giant Engins Matra aerospace concern which had a healthy stake in France's armaments and defence

business. Matra acquired the assets of the Réné Bonnet car company which included a neat little road going sports car called the Djet and, to promote the car's image, established the Matra-Sports sub-division to produce a monocoque F3 car. Thus, almost unwittingly, the task of re-establishing France as an international motorsporting force was fired from the launching pad.

Matra quickly established a reputation for building fine-handling F2 and F3 cars which demonstrated outstandingly good traction. At the same time as Matra was looking to break into F2 at the start of '66, so Ken Tyrrell was looking for a new chassis to replace his existing Coopers. Jackie Stewart, though still contracted to BRM for F1 through to the end of 1967, also had the use of Bourne's F2 engine and a deal was duly done for him to drive a Tyrrell team Matra-BRM in this category throughout the season.

In 1967, still using the Matra chassis, but now powered by the brand new Cosworth FVA engine in the first season of the 1.6-litre F2, Stewart enjoyed considerable success. Meanwhile, a couple of crucial strands were coming together which would result in Matra having a two-pronged F1 World Championship assault for 1968.

The advent of the new Cosworth DFV V8 further facilitated Tyrrell's intention of making the step up into F1 with Jackie Stewart. By the middle of 1967 the Scottish driver had become profoundly disillusioned with BRM's technical performance and was being wooed heavily by Ferrari. But both he and Tyrrell could see that the Cosworth DFV engine offered the greatest potential, and while the Matra engine team was busy developing its own 60-degree V12, Tyrrell put the proposal that his team be allowed to field a Cosworth-engined chassis for Stewart.

One might have expected Matra to administer a lofty rebuff to

such proposals, but in fact the company welcomed the idea with open arms. If the V12 engine should prove troublesome during its first season, at least Matra would gain some worthwhile publicity from the association with Tyrrell and Jackie Stewart. The deal was done.

Thus, the 1968 season saw Jackie Stewart running Cosworth Ford-engined cars from Tyrrell's Surrey lumber yard under the Matra International banner, while the V12-engined cars sallied forth from Matra Sport's base at Velizy to be driven by Jean-Pierre Beltoise. Both teams benefitted from sponsorship from the Elf fuel and lubricants company and ran on Dunlop tyres.

History relates that the Matra-Ford led its very first Grand Prix, Jackie Stewart poking the MS9 F2-based prototype into the lead at the start of the 1968 South African Grand Prix at Kyalami before Jim Clark's Lotus 49 breezed by on the second lap. Clark, of course, was killed before the title battle got into its stride, but Stewart and the definitive Matra MS10 quickly established themselves as the combination to beat.

Unfortunately, Jackie's championship aspirations were dealt a cruel blow when he damaged his wrist in an F2 accident at Jarama, missing the Spanish and Monaco Grands Prix. Beltoise deputised in the Matra International car at the former event, leading before a pit stop to quench an oil leak dropped him to an eventual fifth, while Johnny Servoz-Gavin led from the start at Monte Carlo only to glance a wall and damage a drive-shaft joint in the excitement of the opening lap.

Left: Jean-Pierre Beltoise with the V12 Matra F1 car, 1968.

Right: Jackie Stewart in the F2-based Grand Prix Matra prototype on its debut in South Africa, 1968.

Below right: Beltoise in the V12-engined Matra at Zandvoort, '68.

THE FRENCH CONNECTION

Stewart finally scored his first Matra victory in the Dutch Grand Prix at Zandvoort, still driving with his injured wrist in a plastic cast and making the most of Dunlop's superb wet weather rubber in torrential conditions. Beltoise, now behind the wheel of the V12 MS11, backed that up with a superb second place. Stewart would win again at Nurburgring in conditions even more treacherous, with dense fog exacerbating the torrential rain, and add a third win to his season's tally at Watkins Glen in the US event. But he just lost out in the Championship battle to Graham Hill, although things would be very different the following season.

For 1969, Beltoise joined Stewart in the Matra International line-up as the French team's V12 was confined solely to sports car racing throughout that season. Stewart kicked off the year by taking the old MS10 to victory at Kyalami, then switched to the latest MS80 to reel off wins at Barcelona, Zandvoort, Clermont-Ferrand and Silverstone, before finally clinching his first World Championship with a split-second victory over Rindt's Lotus at Monza.

Yet that title-winning success heralded the end for the Anglo-French partnership. For 1970, Matra planned a renewed assault with its own V12 engine and no longer wanted a Ford-engined machine ranged against it. Stewart tested the Matra V12, but couldn't convince himself it would be a match for the Cosworth-built V8, so a parting of the ways became inevitable. In any event, Jackie was so closely allied with Ford commercially that it was almost unthinkable he would turn his back on the company in the F1 arena.

Tyrrell flirted briefly with March as he laid top secret plans to build his own chassis for the Ford engine in 1970. Matra Sport's new MS120 V12 tackled the Championship program with Beltoise and Henri Pescarolo in the cockpits. But not a single win came the French team's way up until it closed its doors at the end of 1972, although New Zealander Chris Amon, who signed up at the start of 1971, came dramatically close a couple of times.

Although the team scored a hat trick of Le Mans victories between 1972 and 74, providing some consolation for their F1 disappointments, not until 1977 would Matra's V12 engine finally score its first Grand Prix victory. Powering Jacques Laffite's Ligier, it won the Swedish Grand Prix at Anderstorp.

Ligier switched to Cosworth power at the start of 1979, but reverted to the French V12, now under Talbot patronage, for 1981 when Laffite added another two victories finally to rule off the Matra engine's record of Grand Prix achievement.

Above: Beltoise spins at Zandvoort on his way to second place in the 1968 Dutch Grand Prix.

Left: Jackie Stewart's Ford-engined Matra MS10 winning the 1968 Dutch Grand Prix.

Right: Stewart heading for victory in the 1969 French Grand Prix at Clermont-Ferrand in the Matra-Ford MS80.

Stewart and Rindt

Jackie Stewart and Jochen Rindt came from the most disparate of backgrounds and displayed dramatically contrasting styles behind the wheel of a Grand Prix car. Yet for two seasons at the end of the 1960s, these men stood head and shoulders above their rivals as Grand Prix racing's pacemakers, committed rivals on the circuit yet firm friends who lived a few miles from each other near the shores of a Swiss lake.

Statistics show that Stewart was the more successful. Born in the small town of Dumbuck, on the River Clyde, on 10 June 1939, John Young Stewart worked on his father's garage forecourt pumping gas during his youth. But this dyslexic Scot always thought big and, from the moment he first tested a Jaguar E-type at Oulton Park back in 1962, clearly had enormous ability.

Only a year later, the first signs of his Formula 1 potential were graphically illustrated when Ken Tyrrell invited him to test an F3 Cooper-BMC at Goodwood. Within a few laps he was turning quicker times than Cooper's regular Formula 1 team leader Bruce McLaren. Witnesses testify to seeing John Cooper running across the paddock – a sight described as akin to Groucho Marx at speed! – to urge Tyrrell to 'sign that lad up here and now . . .'

Tyrrell didn't need a great deal of encouragement and Jackie's route to Grand Prix stardom was virtually mapped out by the end of that same day. In 1964, Stewart took the British F3 scene by storm, enjoyed a brief test in Jim Clark's F1 Lotus during practice for the British Grand Prix and received an invitation to partner his fellow Scot in Colin Chapman's team for 1965.

Shrewdly, Stewart turned down the offer and joined BRM instead, as Graham Hill's number two. It proved, as so often in

Jackie's career, to be absolutely the right move. He won the 1965 Italian Grand Prix and kicked off 1966 with a fine win at Monaco. Sadly, the over-complexity, and consequent horrendous unreliability, of the new BRM H-16 engine with which the team was preparing to tackle the new 3-litre F1 was to keep Stewart away from the winner's circle for the best part of another two seasons.

Born in Hamburg on 18 April 1942, at the height of the Second World War, Jochen Rindt was orphaned at the age of fifteen months when his parents were killed in a bombing raid. He was raised by his wealthy grandparents in the historic Austrian city of Graz where his family's spice milling business, Klein and Rindt, was situated. History relates that the young Jochen grew up as a real renegade, getting involved in all sorts of youthful scrapes, but demonstrating a fearless turn of speed on everything from skis to mopeds in his pre-motoring infancy.

Jochen also battled to prominence through Formula 3, but raced mostly on the Continent. At the end of 1963, having received his family inheritance when he reached the age of 21, he turned up at the London Racing Car Show and coolly ordered a Formula 2 Brabham which he planned to campaign the following season.

It was on Whit Monday 1964 that the British public became introduced to Jochen Rindt. Driving with an uninhibited and

Opposite page: Rindt hurling his Cooper-Maserati T81 round Monaco in 1967.

Above: Rindt at the wheel of the sensational Lotus 72 en route to victory in the 1970 Dutch Grand Prix.

Right: The sport's only posthumous World Champion.

extrovert brio which was to become his hallmark, he won the Crystal Palace Formula 2 international race, beating Graham Hill into second place in the process. 'Unknown Australian wins at the Palace' roared the headlines in one newspaper. Few would make that mistake again.

He arrived on the Grand Prix scene at the same time as Stewart, although Rindt's 1965 season with Cooper yielded fourth place in the German Grand Prix as its best result. Into the 3-litre formula in 1966, Rindt led the Cooper-Maserati line-up and proved his class by jousting fearlessly with John Surtees's Ferrari for the lead of the rain-soaked Belgian Grand Prix at Spa. He stayed with Cooper to the end of 1967, then switched to Brabham for 1968. By now Stewart had established himself as a consistent winner in the Tyrrell Matra team, but the dynamic Rindt had forged only a reputation for blinding speed and fearlessness during those three years in the Grand Prix arena.

Yet his success in Formula 2, where he remained undisputed king, continued to serve as a true index of his ability. And Stewart knew in his heart that, should Jochen get himself into a reliably competitive car, he would become a formidable adversary.

In the wake of Jimmy Clark's death, Colin Chapman approached Rindt to drive for Lotus at the start of 1969. This seemed just the break he needed, but initially the results seemed reluctant to flow. Denis Jenkinson, respected Continental Correspondent of *Motor Sport* magazine, staked his beard that Rindt would never win a Grand Prix. For a time, it seemed as though that hirsute appendage was safe!

The 1969 British Grand Prix at Silverstone finally produced the expected titanic battle between Stewart's Tyrrell Matra MS80 and Rindt's Lotus 49B. This spell-binding two car confrontation saw Rindt hold the upper hand for most of the distance, only to be thwarted first by a loose rear wing end plate, then by shortage of fuel. He finished a dejected fourth, telling Chapman in no uncertain terms what he thought about his

team's standards of car preparation. The Lotus boss and his new star driver always had a somewhat tense relationship, Jochen's aggressive and outspoken attitude contrasting sharply with the harmony Chapman had enjoyed with the late Jim Clark.

At Monza, Stewart and Rindt renewed their battle, Stewart just taking victory by half a length to clinch his first World Championship. Finally, at Watkins Glen, Denis Jenkinson's beard received its death sentence. Rindt won the United States Grand Prix in fine style, exorcising the spell that had seemed to be hanging over him ever since his arrival on the F1 scene.

In 1970, the tables were turned between Stewart and Rindt. Jochen now benefitted from the sensational new Lotus 72 while Stewart was handicapped with the March 701, very much an interim move for the Tyrrell team which was building its new car in conditions of great secrecy. Jochen added to his victory tally with a stupendous last corner win at Monaco with the Lotus 49, then added a further four momentous victories to his tally with the new type 72.

At last the tempestuous Austrian seemed to have cast aside his 'wild boy' persona. His driving style assumed a polish and finesse hitherto lacking. Yet he was to be denied knowledge of his greatest achievement. Just twenty seven years old and poised on the brink of the World Championship, Jochen was killed in practice for the Italian Grand Prix at Monza. He would become the sport's only posthumous Champion.

Coming at the end of a season which had also seen the death of Piers Courage, Rindt's loss was a traumatic blow for Stewart who seriously considered retiring. But the Scot would race on to add the 1971 and 73 World Championships to his '69 title before quitting the cockpit, healthy and unharmed, at the end of 1973.

Yet Jackie would always look back and think on what might have happened in 1971. 'Had he survived, whatever cars the rest of us drove, I think the number one challenge would have still been beating Jochen,' he later reflected.

Above left: Stewart's Matra MS80 leads Rindt's Lotus 49C during their titanic battle for the lead of the 1969 British Grand Prix.

Above: Stewart winning the 1968 Dutch Grand Prix with the Matra MS10.

Right: John Young Stewart, close friend and rival of Jochen Rindt.

Part 4

The 1970s

Chapman Re-writes the Rules

Having broken fresh ground in Grand Prix car design with the Cosworth Ford-engined Lotus 49, introduced in 1967, Colin Chapman demanded a more radical and sophisticated chassis when it came to conceiving a replacement for this epochal racing car. Formula 1 had ventured up a technical blind alley in 1969 with several teams, including Lotus, trying four-wheel-drive systems, but it quickly became clear that a lightweight rear-wheel-drive package remained the best solution at a time when increasing aerodynamic downforce was being developed from front and rear aerofoils.

Early in 1970, the wraps came off the stunning new Lotus type 72. Fitted with a Cosworth-Ford engine, that was pretty well where its similarity to most of the opposition started and finished. This sleek chisel-nosed challenger sported such trend-setting niceties as side water radiators, inboard brakes all round for lower unsprung weight and rising rate torsion bar suspension. It was intended to make maximum use of Firestone's latest range of lighter construction racing tyres and be capable of running further and faster on softer compounds.

The abrasive Jochen Rindt, having now come to terms with Chapman's personal methodology, realised this was the car that could finally unlock the World Championship for him. But the Lotus 72 had a troubled debut, its chassis being extensively re-vamped and stiffened after the first few races. But once properly sorted, Rindt made it absolutely fly.

Having used the obsolete Lotus 49C to win at Monaco, Rindt now reeled off victories at Zandvoort, Clermont-Ferrand,

Brands Hatch and Hockenheim before tragically crashing fatally at Monza, almost certainly due to a fracture of an inboard front brake shaft. Not for the first time Chapman and Lotus would find themselves embroiled in an Italian legal controversy, raising unfortunate echoes of Clark's inadvertent involvement in the von Trips tragedy some nine years before.

Lotus' 'junior' driver Emerson Fittipaldi was now promoted to the full-time F1 team, restoring morale with a well-judged run to victory in the United States Grand Prix – only his fourth F1 outing! Fittipaldi would stay on for another three years and, although the Lotus 72 would not win a race in 1971, in 1972 the young Brazilian returned it to a position of pre-eminence. At 25 years old, he used Chapman's baby to become the youngest World Champion in the history of the sport.

Chapman was always one to have the two best drivers he could possibly find, so after a disappointing spell with some less-than-competitive number twos, he set Fittipaldi bristling by signing up the dynamic Ronnie Peterson at the start of 1973. For three years the young Swede had been driving for the fledgling March team, and while Chapman had regularly tempted him with attractive offers, his March contract was water-tight. But it expired at the end of '72 after which Peterson was welcomed into the Lotus fold with open arms.

Between them, Fittipaldi and Peterson, now on Goodyear rubber, won seven Grands Prix in 1973. But although they clinched the Constructors' title for Team Lotus, by dividing up the race wins they allowed Jackie Stewart through to take his third

Previous page: Emerson Fittipaldi wins the 1975 British Grand Prix in the McLaren M23 – the last F1 victory of the Brazilian's career.

Left: Prelude to disaster. Rindt in the Lotus 72, minus nose and tail wings, a couple of laps before he crashed fatally at Parabolica, this very spot, during practice for the 1970 Italian Grand Prix.

Above: Ronnie Peterson in the Lotus 72, the classic combination of 1973.

Right: Graham Hill gives the prototype Lotus 72 a test outing on the runway adjacent to the team's headquarters at Hethel, Norfolk.

Drivers' Championship. By the end of the year Chapman was champing at the bit to produce a replacement which would incorporate all the 72's best attributes, but built round a chassis some 100 pounds lighter . . .

The result of this ambitious thinking was the Lotus 76, complete with an over-complex electro-hydraulic clutch actuation system. The car was a failure, proving heavy and unreliable, so the faithful type 72s were dusted down and brought back to the

front line of F1 action. Peterson's dazzling car control produced three more Grand Prix victories at Monaco, Dijon-Prenois and Monza, while new team-mate Jacky Ickx demonstrated his legendary wet weather flair to beat Niki Lauda's Ferrari in the Brands Hatch Race of Champions.

The Lotus 72 always proved extremely sensitive to tyre specification and, towards the end of the 1974 season, Peterson increasingly voiced complaints about the understeer that he was experiencing on Goodyear's latest rubber. It was only understandable that the tyre supplier should tailor its latest products to suit the characteristics of the most competitive cars of the moment. Unfortunately, the Lotus 72 no longer fell into this elite category which was now monopolised by McLaren's M23 and the new breed of flat-12 Ferrari.

Peterson struggled through 1975 with a succession of stand-in team-mates who appeared on the scene after Ickx threw in the towel and retired from F1 mid-season. This glorious car's final outing came in the 1975 United States Grand Prix at Watkins Glen and, even then, Peterson still managed to haul it home in the points, finishing a remarkable fifth.

Six seasons had passed since the prototype Lotus 72 first ventured out on to the circuit. In the intervening years it had won no fewer than twenty Grands Prix in the hands of Rindt, Fittipaldi and Peterson as well as three Constructors' Championship titles for Team Lotus (1970, 72 and 73). It had nobly earned its position in history as one of the greatest Grand Prix cars of all time.

Top: Fittipaldi triumphs in the 1972 Belgian Grand Prix at Nivelles – in a Lotus 72.

Above left: Jochen Rindt winning the 1970 French Grand Prix again in the Lotus 72.

Left: Ronnie Peterson heads for victory at Monaco four years later.

Right: Graham Hill en route to the fourth of his five Monaco Grand Prix victories – 1968, Lotus 49B.

The Heyday of Elf Team Tyrrell

It was an abiding enthusiasm for soccer which started Surrey timber merchant Ken Tyrrell out on the long road to becoming the constructor of the cars used by Jackie Stewart to win two World Championship titles in the early 1970s. Back in the late 1940s, Ken's local soccer club arranged a trip to Silverstone. Ken went along and was instantly attracted to the sport of motor racing, particularly fascinated by the 500cc Formula 3 event which was included on the supporting programme.

It was not long before Ken bought himself a part share in an F3 Cooper-Norton. His first race outing came at Snetterton in 1952, after which he became one of this close-fought category's leading lights over the six seasons that followed. But despite winning an international race at Karkskoga, in Sweden, Ken came to realise that he was never going to make the front rank.

Better by far, he reasoned, to make a real success of team management and organisation rather than competing behind the wheel as an also-ran. In 1960, the Tyrrell Racing Team was established to run the factory-supported 1100cc Formula Junior Coopers for Henry Taylor and Keith Ballisat, later to become competitions managers for Ford and Shell respectively. But it was in late 1963 that Tyrrell struck up the relationship that would help carry him to the forefront of F1 success.

Jackie Stewart made a sensational impression testing an F3

Cooper at Goodwood and was quickly signed up by Ken for 1964, the season in which the young Scot would dominate the British F3 scene. Although Jackie graduated to F1 with BRM, Tyrrell kept his services for F2 over the next few years and he was only too keen to join Ken in F1 at the start of 1968 as part of the Cosworth-Ford powered Matra International team.

As recounted elsewhere, after Tyrrell won them the Championship in 1969, Matra chose to concentrate on its own V12-engined cars for the 1970 season, effectively leaving Tyrrell out on a limb. Ken investigated possible deals to run either a McLaren or Brabham chassis for Stewart, but both those teams were contracted to Goodyear who clearly would not have been too happy to see a private car being sold to Tyrrell with the very real risk that Jackie would beat them using Dunlops.

In the event, Ken found himself backed into a position where he had no alternative but to buy three of the new March 701s on offer from the newly established Bicester-based constructor. But even as Stewart was testing the first Tyrrell 701 at Silverstone in February 1970, Ken was setting in place plans to ensure his team's complete independence. He had decided that he would build his own Grand Prix car and that it would make its debut in the Oulton Park Gold Cup meeting on 22 August 1970.

This pressing deadline, set immutably by the demands of

Right: Stewart's Matra MS80 leads the Brabham of Jacky Ickx during the 1969 Canadian Grand Prix. Ickx ran into the back of Stewart's car, eliminating the Scot from the race.

Below: The start of the Canadian race with Rindt's Lotus 49B just getting the jump on Ickx, the Matras of Stewart and Beltoise, and Siffert's Lotus 49C (9).

Below right: Typically Tyrrell. Jackie Stewart takes the flag to win the 1971 British Grand Prix at Silverstone.

Left: As an interim measure to fill the gap between Matra and his own car, Tyrrell ran this March for Jackie Stewart.

Right and below left: Stewart heads for a memorable victory at Monaco, 1971, despite having almost no braking effect on the rear wheels.

Below right: Jackie's last victory. On the rostrum at Nurburgring after the 1973 German Grand Prix.

future sponsorship negotiations, was impressed by Tyrrell in his preliminary meeting with Derek Gardner, the man the team owner had targeted to design the new car. Gardner had previously been a key engineer with Ferguson who manufactured the four-wheel-drive system for the Matra MS84 Grand Prix car which Stewart had tested briefly during 1969 and which was raced to sixth place in that year's Canadian Grand Prix by Johnny Servoz-Gavin. What Tyrrell had seen of Gardner's work impressed him very much, so now Tyrrell offered him the chance of his career.

The mock-up of the first Tyrrell chassis was built in conditions of great secrecy in the garage at Gardner's home in Leamington Spa, Stewart even flying up for a preliminary seat fitting in these unlikely surroundings. The project to produce the first prototype cost £22,500 – big money by the standards of the time, but

quickly to look like small change as F1 budget inflation spiralled dramatically throughout the following decade.

Tyrrell 001, a neatly conceived 'bath tub' monocoque chassis with distinctively bulbous side panels to accommodate its fuel cells, was unveiled at Ford's London base in Regent Street on 17 August, 1970. On its first race outing, at Oulton Park as scheduled, Stewart shattered the lap record and led commandingly before its throttle jammed. No victories would await the new car during its first half-season, but it would comfortably out-run its opposition in the Canadian and United States Grands Prix before retiring.

For 1971, the team switched to Goodyear rubber and would enter Stewart and rising star François Cevert under the Elf Team Tyrrell banner, recognising the sponsorship provided by the French fuel company. Once into his stride, there was no stopping Stewart and the new Tyrrell. The irrepressible Scot stormed to victory in the Spanish, Monaco, French, British, German and Canadian Grands Prix to clinch his second Championship in overwhelming style. And when Stewart faded to fifth place with handling problems at Watkins Glen, Cevert picked up the reins to score what was to be the sole victory of his tragically short Grand Prix career.

The original Tyrrell design had been viewed by Gardner as an essentially short-term concept, and during 1971 he completed the preliminary outline of a second generation concept which finally metamorphosed into the lower and shorter 005/006 range which was originally designed to use inboard front brakes as a means of further reducing unsprung weight. Cevert crashed the first prototype during practice for the French Grand Prix at Clermont-Ferrand, this being just one of a catalogue of niggling incidents which prevented the team from retaining its hard-won Championship.

For a start, the helter-skelter existence sustained by Stewart over the past few years, combining intense off-track business and promotional activities with a competitive racing pro-

Left: François Cevert was a splendid team-mate to Stewart throughout much of his Tyrrell career. Here the Frenchman heads towards second place in his home Grand Prix in 1971.

Below left: Stewart takes the flag to win the 1973 German Grand Prix.

Bottom left: Cevert shadows Stewart during the 1973 German Grand Prix. After the race, Jackie conceded 'François could have passed me any time he liked."

Below right: Carlos Pace (left) won the 1975 Brazilian Grand Prix at Interlagos, a circuit which now bears his name. He was tragically killed in an air crash at the start of 1977. Emerson Fittipaldi (right) was the man who really put Brazil on the F1 motor racing map.

gramme, caught up with the Scot in a big way during the first half of the year. A duodenal ulcer was diagnosed and he was obliged to miss the Belgian Grand Prix at Nivelles, but bounced back with a well-judged win in the French race at Clermont-Ferrand, then chased Fittipaldi's Lotus home in second place at Brands Hatch, a circuit on which he was never quite able to make any Tyrrell behave properly over the ripples and bumps.

Stewart gave the new Tyrrell 005 its first race at Osterreich-ring, where outboard brakes had been installed after continued vibration problems beset the original inboard set-up, but erratic tyre wear dropped him from an initial commanding lead to a frustrated seventh at the chequered flag. His clutch burned out on the grid at Monza, but Stewart rounded off the season in fine form with wins in Canada and the United States. However, Emerson Fittipaldi had long since clinched the World Championship for himself and Team Lotus.

At the start of the 1973 season, Stewart confided in Tyrrell that he had decided to retire at the end of the season, but embarked on his final Championship assault with characteristic gusto. Using essentially the same cars, the monocoques of which were clad with mandatory deformable structures from the Spanish Grand Prix onwards, Stewart's sheer driving flair enabled him to compete with the better handling Lotus 72s now driven by Fittipaldi and Peterson.

He won at Kyalami, Zolder, Monaco, Zandvoort and the Nurburgring, shadowed home in the last two events by Cevert in second place. Privately, he acknowledged to Tyrrell that 'François is now faster than me. In the German Grand Prix he could have passed me anytime he wanted to . . .' That would be Stewart's final Grand Prix success, establishing a new record of 27 career wins that would stand for another 14 years before being toppled by Alain Prost.

Tragically, Cevert was killed at Watkins Glen practising for the United States Grand Prix and Tyrrell withdrew the team's two other entries, those of Stewart and Chris Amon, from the race. A great driving partnership had come to an end and the Tyrrell team would never again scale such dramatic heights of achievement.

The Boys from Brazil

Just as Fangio and Gonzales had put Argentina on the motor racing map in the fifties, and the Rodriguez brothers had done the same for Mexico in the sixties, the arrival of Emerson Fittipaldi on the Grand Prix scene in 1970 opened a floodgate of Brazilian talent which is still in full flow with Ayrton Senna and Nelson Piquet twenty years later.

The son of Wilson Fittipaldi, a well-known and highly respected Brazilian motorsports journalist and commentator who had covered Fangio's European F1 assault in the early 1950s, Emerson was born in Sao Paulo on 12 December, 1946. He and his elder brother Wilson Jnr raced motorcycles and karts in their early teens and Emerson won the 1967 Brazilian Formula Vee championship before coming to Britain to race in Formula Ford two years later.

His progress proved meteoric. Within sixteen months, he had mastered this junior category, graduated through Formula 3 with honours and in 1970 embarked on a European Formula 2 Championship campaign in that hotly contested holding area

for future Grand Prix talent. Offered his Grand Prix debut by Lotus in the 1970 British Grand Prix at the wheel of an outdated Lotus 49C, he kept it out of trouble to finish eighth, and then brought it home fourth in the German Grand Prix at Hockenheim, both these races being won by Rindt's Lotus 72.

Propelled into the role of team leadership after the Austrian's tragic death at Monza, Fittipaldi and Team Lotus struggled slightly in 1971 during which Emerson was badly shaken up by a serious road accident in France. But his increasing maturity and assurance helped him forge a productive rapport with Colin Chapman and, to watch Emerson reel off six confident victories on his way to becoming the youngest World Champion ever in 1972, was to see at work an unflustered natural talent which many were tempted to compare with Jim Clark's.

By the start of the 1972 season, there would be no fewer than three Brazilians contesting the World Championship, brother Wilson having secured a sponsored place in Bernie Ecclestone's resurgent Brabham team while Jose Carlos Pace was signed up

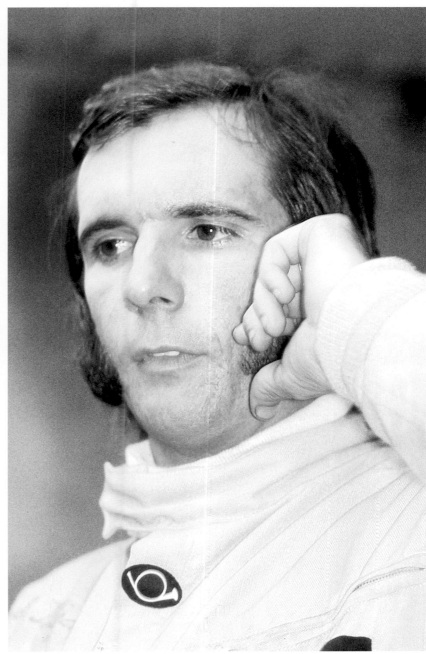

Left: Fittipaldi's McLaren leads Niki Lauda's Ferrari during Fittipaldi's winning drive in Belgium, 1974. Earlier that year (*below left*), he had won on home ground at Interlagos.

Right: Pace struggling manfully with the Brabham-Alfa Romeo BT45, Monaco, 1976.

Below: Pace at speed with the winning Brabham-Cosworth BT44B.

with Frank Williams and would later join Team Surtees. Having two Fittipaldis in F1 was almost more than the fanatical Brazilians could cope with, and when Wilson and Emerson completed the first lap of that year's non-championship F1 race at Sao Paulo's spectacular Interlagos circuit in first and second positions, Wilson Fittipaldi Senior's commentary could have been heard without the aid of any public address system!

Emerson was wary of the way in which Colin Chapman recruited Ronnie Peterson to Team Lotus alongside him in 1973

and shrewdly switched to the Marlboro McLaren line-up the following year. In a season which would see him bring all his experience and strategy to bear, Fittipaldi cemented this new partnership with wins in the Brazilian, Belgian and Canadian Grands Prix to clinch his second World Championship.

Fittipaldi's ultra-smooth driving style made it almost look as if his cars were running on rails and this undramatic economy of outward effort saw him finish second in the Championship to Lauda in 1975. His career subsequently became side-tracked when he agreed to join the 'family' F1 team which had been established by brother Wilson during 1975 with considerable sponsorship from the Brazilian-based Copersucar sugar producing cartel. But by allowing emotion to rule sound motor racing judgement, Emerson Fittipaldi effectively wiped out a highly promising Grand Prix career at the age of 29.

Ahead of him lay five seasons of dogged and unproductive toil, highlighted only by a glorious run into second place in the 1978 Brazilian Grand Prix at Rio. By the start of 1980 he had lost his touch as a driver and Fittipaldi Automotive, as the team was now titled, floundered as the money and motivation ran short.

At the end of 1980, Emerson quit the cockpit and took over the role of team manager leaving the driving to fellow Brazilian Chico Serra and fast Finn Keke Rosberg. But the big sponsor they had been angling for never came about and, after struggling through 1982 with a single car for Serra, Fittipaldi Automotive closed its doors at the end of that season.

Wilson Fittipaldi never won a Grand Prix and retired from active driving at the end of 1975 after steering the Copersucar through a somewhat lurid pilot season. Today he looks after the family's extensive business interests, which include a Mercedes-Benz dealership and a 200,000 acre orange plantation, in his native Brazil.

Carlos Pace, after a disappointing time with Team Surtees,

switched to the Brabham team in the middle of 1974 and rounded off that season with a strong second place in the United States Grand Prix. Winner of the 1975 Brazilian Grand Prix, where he beat Fittipaldi's McLaren in a straight fight, he was killed in a light aircraft crash a few weeks prior to the start of the 1977 European Grand Prix season.

The 1982 closure was not the last the racing world had heard of Emerson, however. After a brief lay-off, he returned to the US domestic sports car scene and then, in 1984, moved into the highly competitive Indy car arena at the wheel of a March-Cosworth 84C. He won his first Indy car triumph with a 40 second victory over Al Unser in the 1985 Michigan 500, triumphed at Elkhart Lake the following year and then scored two wins apiece during the 1987 and 88 seasons.

In 1989, at the wheel of a Marlboro-backed Patrick Racing Penske PC19, powered by an Ilmor/Chevrolet V8, Emerson Fittipaldi not only became the first non-American to win the CART Championship, but also became the first F1 champion since Mario Andretti to win the Indianapolis 500. At 42 years old, he was driving with as much apparent skill and determination as ever.

Left: Nelson Piquet scores his first victory, Long Beach, 1980, with the Brabham BT49.

Below: Pace celebrates his victory at Interlagos with Fittipaldi and Jochen Mass, 1975 Brazilian Grand Prix.

Right: James Hunt (*above*) helped put Hesketh Racing on the map, but the rubber-suspended Hesketh 308E (*below*) helped sink the team at the end of 1975.

A Lordly Effort

Hesketh Racing may, from the outside, have seemed all about a group of chums who decided to have a crack at Formula 1 as something of a jolly jape, but in fact the enthusiastic little team achieved a good deal, including James Hunt's maiden Grand Prix victory, on an extremely limited budget.

Alexander Fermor-Hesketh, whose family seat, Easton Neston, was situated in Towcester, just a few miles from Silverstone, was first seduced into supporting a racing team by his friend Anthony Horsley, a close friend of Frank Williams from the time they both used to race F3 cars together in the early 1960s. Horsley, whose nickname had been 'Bubbles' ever since anybody could recall, made a return to F3 in early 1972 at the wheel of a Dastle car entered under the Hesketh banner.

It did not take long for Horsley to conclude that race driving was hardly his metier; he opted for team management duties and the team recruited the youthful James Hunt whose career was then going through something of a depression, having recently been dropped from the works STP March F3 team. Encouraged by his determination, Hesketh acquired an F2 March 712M for James to handle towards the end of the year and it quickly became clear that the Englishman had some definite long-term potential.

Things moved fast in Hesketh Racing circles. It was initially decided to launch a full-blown assault on the European F2 Championship with a new Surtees TS15 during 1973 and Hesketh also hired James an F1 Surtees TS9B in which he made his F1 debut, finishing third in the non-title Brands Hatch Race of Champions. Soon after, Hesketh and his men thought, 'heck, let's go the whole hog.' The Surtees project was abandoned, the team

Above: James' Hesketh March 731 heads for a splendid third place in the 1973 Dutch Grand Prix at Zandvoort.

Below: Alexander Hesketh ushers his driver to the rostrum, Zandvoort, 1973.

Right and above right: These two shots show Hunt heading for a splendid second place to Peterson's Lotus 72 in the 1973 United States Grand Prix at Watkins Glen.

leased an F1 March 731 and threw itself wholeheartedly into the World Championship battle.

Its car turned out in a distinctive, patriotic, red, white and blue livery, the Hesketh team exuded an extrovert, slightly frivolous mood with helicopters, parties and Porsches as seemingly indispensible adjuncts to the main business of the day. But if Alexander cut a slightly comic-book image, there was absolutely nothing frivolous about his team's approach to F1. Horsley and newly recruited former March engineer Harvey

Postlethwaite did a fine job fielding that 731, easily eclipsing the factory car's efforts, and Hunt had clearly cast aside his early reputation as an unpredictable performer.

Only engine failure prevented the team from scoring Championship points at Monaco, but James was sixth at Paul Ricard and then a sensational fourth in the British Grand Prix at Silverstone, the Hesketh March crossing the line close behind Peter Revson's winning McLaren M23, Ronnie Peterson's Lotus 72 and Denny Hulme's M23. James went on to finish third at Zandvoort, then topped off the season with a magnificent run to second place in the US Grand Prix at Watkins Glen, only feet behind Peterson's winning Lotus.

Harvey Postlethwaite harnessed all his aerodynamic knowhow to produce the first Hesketh 308 in time for the 1975 season, this being a relatively conventional Cosworth-Ford engined machine which drew on the many technical lessons learned with the March 731. James raised hopes by qualifying the 308 on pole position for the Race of Champions, but severe handling problems on his Firestone rubber in the torrential conditions prevailing on race day prompted his retirement. But he did win Alexander's local F1 race, the Silverstone International Trophy, after an early battle with Ronnie Peterson's troublesome Lotus 76.

Out on the World Championship trail, the Hesketh 308 was beset by mechanical unreliability, but third places in both Sweden and Austria were encouraging, and the season ended with a fourth in Canada and a third at Watkins Glen, chasing home the two Brabham BT44s of Carlos Reutemann and Carlos Pace. By this time the 308 had been heavily revamped with side water radiators and a full-width nose aerofoil, but Postlethwaite had some even more ambitious design plans up his sleeve for

Left: Lord Hesketh helps James and Ronnie Peterson celebrate on the rostrum at Watkins Glen after the epic 1973 US Grand Prix chase.

Below: Hunt steering the Hesketh 308C to the team's lone Grand Prix victory, Zandvoort, 1975.

Lower left: The pit signal shows that James has over ten seconds in hand over Lauda's Ferrari at this stage of the '75 Dutch Grand Prix.

Below right: Niki Lauda would involuntarily become a Grand Prix hero in 1976.

Below, far right: He showers champagne after winning the '74 Dutch Grand Prix, two years prior to his dreadful accident at the Nurburgring.

1975 in the guise of the 308C which was originally designed with rubber cone suspension which had been tested from time to time on the original car. But the realities of financial pressure were beginning to impinge on the Hesketh team and, without serious commercial sponsorship, it was clear that Alexander could not continue indefinitely picking up the fast-mushrooming tab.

The signs that the future was anything but secure had become clear even before Hunt scored the marque's lone Grand Prix victory, a nail-biting win over Niki Lauda's Ferrari 312T in the Dutch Grand Prix at Zandvoort. The team made maximum use of the wet/dry track conditions, playing their tactics to perfection, and leaving James with the task of sustaining an intense bout of pressure from the Austrian who was fast becoming the most respected F1 performer of his era. That Hunt remained totally unflustered by the Ferrari team leader's presence in his mirrors provided a useful pointer to the Englishman's future form.

At the end of the season, Alexander revealed that 'The Biggest Little Team in the World' had been unable to raise the necessary backing to continue. Many believed his efforts to find sponsorship had been less than energetic. The team would continue building cars for rental to those who could produce the necessary backing, but the halcyon days of James Hunt and Hesketh Racing had run their course.

Lauda and Ferrari

The combination of Niki Lauda and Ferrari may have seemed an unlikely one to those who watched the buck-toothed Austrian youngster floundering around at the back of the field during his 1972 season as a Grand Prix debutant. But the doubters under-estimated Niki's singlemindedness, determination and sheer calculating efficiency. He was a man who knew precisely where he wanted to go and made sure that the Ferrari team got the message just how much it needed him.

The first few seasons of the decade had seen the famous Maranello team turn in some patchy performances. The 1970 season had promised a great deal with Belgium's Jacky Ickx challenging strongly for the Championship at the wheel of the 3-litre flat-12 cylinder 312B1, just losing out to the late Jochen Rindt despite scoring three commanding wins in the second half of the season.

For the next two years, Ferrari fortunes slipped noticeably and, with plans to run only one car in 1973, Regazzoni was released to drive for BRM. There the Swiss found himself teamed up with young Lauda. The Austrian had seemingly mortgaged his life away getting into F1 with March for that abortive F1 season, but now successfully infiltrated the BRM ranks with promises that he would bring along outside sponsorship. In the event, this was not forthcoming, but team director Louis Stanley, brother-in-law of the incapacitated Sir Alfred Owen, agreed to keep him on if he would sign a contract for the following two seasons.

Niki had no choice but to reach for his pen, but, equally, felt he had no alternative but to accept an offer from Ferrari when Regazzoni recommended to the Commendatore that the Austrian new boy accompanied him back to Maranello for the start of the 1974 season. The lawyers eventually sorted the severance of his contract with BRM, but from Lauda's career viewpoint it was absolutely the right move.

With the Ferrari team's effort now monitored with a refreshing objectivity by Luca Montezemolo, a member of the Fiat-controlling Agnelli dynasty, a great deal of progress was made in 1974. Technical director, Mauro Forghieri made considerable improvements to the 312B3 chassis and flat-12 engine which now developed some 25bhp more than the Cosworth DFV used by most of the opposition. This enabled Lauda to win both the Spanish and Dutch Grands Prix in convincing style.

Only Lauda's relative inexperience of running at the front of the field deprived him of other wins in Germany (crashed on the first lap) and Canada (crashed in the closing stages after leading) and an unfortunate punctured tyre cost him a win in the British race at Brands Hatch. Even so, he remained a contender for the World Championship right through to the last race of the year before canny McLaren team leader Emerson Fittipaldi nipped through to take the title.

Having now found his feet and harnessed the Ferrari system to work for him, Lauda embarked on a successful World Championship assault in 1975. Forghieri pencilled a totally new car,

the old car, but then broke a rib in a tractor accident in the grounds of his Austrian lakeside home. This injury handicapped his performance in the Spanish Grand Prix where Hunt won, only to be disqualified for dimensional infringement of his car's rear track, and while further victories in Belgium and Monaco tended to suggest Lauda was near-invincible, the script went very badly wrong in the second half of the season.

Grappling mid-field on a treacherously rain-slicked Nurburgring during the early stages of the German Grand Prix, Niki's Ferrari snapped out of control and crashed heavily, almost certainly due to a suspension breakage. The car erupted in flames and it was only thanks to the outstanding bravery of fellow drivers Brett Lunger, Arturo Merzario and Guy Edwards, plus a nearby track marshal, that he did not die in the inferno.

He was immediately rushed to hospital where the doctors feared as much for his scorched lungs as the unsightly burns to his head and face. Initially he seemed in a parlous state and the Last Rites of the Catholic Church were administered at his bedside. The sheer terror of this event had a fundamental mental impact on Lauda, triggering a remarkable fight back from his injuries. Only six weeks after that miraculous escape, he reappeared in the pit lane at Monza, head swathed in bandages beneath his helmet.

the fine-handling 312T, which featured a transverse gearbox situated ahead of the rear axle line for enhanced traction and balance. Lauda's meticulous and mechanically sympathetic driving style extracted the absolute maximum from the new machine which propelled him to victory in the Monaco, Belgian, Swedish, French and United States Grands Prix, the Austrian emerging triumphantly as World Champion in what was only his fourth F1 season.

For 1976 Ferrari relied on an uprated version of the 312T, but although Niki started well enough it was soon clear that the combination of James Hunt and the McLaren M23 would take a great deal of beating. Lauda won in Brazil and South Africa with

Above left: Niki Lauda, post-accident.

Top: After winning the 1975 Swedish Grand Prix.

Left: Taking the Ferrari 312B/3 to victory in the 1974 Dutch Grand Prix.

Above right: Keeping away from the kerbs to win at Monaco, 1975.

Right: On his brave return to the cockpit at Monza, 1976, only six weeks after his life-threatening accident.

Above: Lauda seizes the lead of the '77 South African Grand Prix from James Hunt's McLaren.

Above right: Mechanics acknowledge with delight Niki's win in the 1977 South African Grand Prix.

Left: With the Ferrari 312T2 aiming for victory in the 1977 Dutch Grand Prix, his last win for the Maranello team.

Right: After winning the 1977 German Grand Prix at Hockenheim – one year after his terrible accident.

In a display of objective detachment and considerable courage, Lauda stormed to fourth place on his comeback drive to signal that he had not completely given up hope of retaining his Championship, forcing James Hunt on to the defensive. The battle would go down to the wire at a rain-soaked Japanese Grand Prix at Mount Fuji where Lauda pulled out, making no bones about the fact that he thought the conditions were unacceptably dangerous.

The Italians deify their racing drivers, so Lauda was not easily to be forgiven by Ferrari for what was commonly perceived as cowardice in action. With Argentinian Carlos Reutemann joining the team for 1977, most critics expected Niki to fulfil an insignificant supporting role. But Lauda had other ideas.

After Reutemann won the second race of the season in Brazil, Lauda seized the initiative and demanded to take charge of the test programme once again. Test and development work had proved his forte during his three seasons with Maranello and, in an intensive bout at Kyalami prior to the South African race, he successfully regained the initiative within the team.

After he won at South Africa, Lauda received an effusive telegram of congratulations from Enzo Ferrari. But Lauda recalled only too well the lukewarm response he had received from the Commendatore when he had telephoned Maranello to explain the events at Mount Fuji only three months earlier. Niki knew that his time with the famous Italian team was coming to an end.

He would win two more races that season – Germany and Holland – before clinching his second championship title with a fourth place finish at Watkins Glen. He then walked out on the team, leaving them in the lurch for the last two races, pleading a sudden bout of flu.

Many observers poured scorn on what they regarded as unacceptable behaviour from a man who prided himself on his professional approach. Niki saw it as getting even, scoring a point over Old Man Ferrari at a crucial moment. And not many people were sharp enough to outflank the Commendatore.

Master James and McLaren

Success in Formula 1 so frequently depends on the right person being in the right place at the right time, a lesson James Hunt would learn to his own considerable benefit at the end of the 1975 World Championship season. James had made the headlines in the summer of '75 when he steered his Hesketh 308 to a close victory over Niki Lauda's more powerful Ferrari 312T in the Dutch Grand Prix at Zandvoort, but since that memorable afternoon his Lordship's team had lost much of its competitive momentum.

A couple of months later it was becoming clear that lack of forthcoming sponsorship would force Hesketh to shut up shop at the end of the year, but Hunt was not unduly bothered. He had received tentative offers both from Brabham and Lotus, but, more interestingly, James had heard on the F1 grapevine that Emerson Fittipaldi had yet to sign his contract with the Marlboro McLaren team for 1976.

Three days before the announcement that Fittipaldi was to join his brother Wilson driving for their own Copersucar organisation, Emerson's manager telephoned James to tip him off that the Brazilian driver would not be staying on with McLaren. Up to that point Hunt and McLaren had kept in touch 'just in case' and, within minutes of McLaren team manager Teddy Mayer hearing the news from Fittipaldi, he was on to James like a flash. Within 36 hours, the deal was done for Hunt to drive a Marlboro McLaren in 1976.

Although James sometimes tended to display the sort of extrovert high spirits which reflected the least appealing side of the British public school ethos, there could be no doubt that he had

finally shrugged off the 'crasher' label which dogged his early years as a professional racer. Facing the 1976 season from the cockpit of the highly competitive Cosworth-engined McLaren M23, the 28-year old Englishman was at the absolute zenith of his career. That final season with Hesketh had finally enabled him to mature into a genuine top-line contender.

From the outset, James stamped his authority on the team, demoralising resident team-mate Jochen Mass by qualifying on pole position for the Brazilian Grand Prix at Interlagos. He did

Above left and left: Hunt's McLaren M23 winning the 1976 French Grand Prix at Paul Ricard.

Above: Triumph at Watkins Glen in the '76 US Grand Prix, clawing ever closer to the title.

Right: The McLaren team urge on their man from the pit wall.

Left: Back at the Glen again, this time winning the '77 US Grand Prix in the McLaren M26.

Below: In the Harvey Postlethwaite-designed Wolf WR9, early 1979.

Right: Last time out. James in the Wolf practising for the 1979 Monaco Grand Prix. Within a week, he quit racing for good . . .

not finish this race, but ran commandingly with the leading bunch before his retirement. He was second to Lauda's Ferrari in South Africa, retired at Long Beach, but won both the non-title Brands Hatch Race of Champions and Silverstone International Trophy curtain raisers prior to the European season.

While there was not much wrong with James's driving, the McLaren team found itself at the centre of two crucial disqualification dramas during the course of the season. After winning the Spanish Grand Prix at Jarama, James found himself disqualified when the M23's rear track was decreed fractionally too wide at post-race scrutineering. The team was reinstated on appeal, but when a first corner multiple accident resulted in the British Grand Prix being stopped, it was later deemed that Hunt's participation in the re-start was illegal.

Although he won the race on the road, James was later deprived of that morale-boosting home success, but it would have been a brave official who would have dared order his McLaren off the Brands Hatch grid in front of the fiercely partisan crowd who demonstrated their support for Hunt with untypically vociferous roars of approval from the grandstand. In that respect, James captured the mood of the moment and became something of a national hero.

It was only after Niki Lauda's return to the cockpit following his fiery Nurburgring accident that FISA bureaucracy finally decreed that Hunt would be stripped of his British Grand Prix triumph. With only three races still left to run, James suddenly found his points deficit to Lauda increased from eight to seventeen. Yet he rose to the challenge, winning both the Canadian and United States races in commanding style and then grasping the title by a single point in a nerve-wracking Japanese finale which saw Lauda pull out of the rain-soaked race and James recover to take a crucial third place after a late-race stop to fit fresh rubber after a tyre deflated.

It seemed more than likely Hunt could retain his title in '77, armed first with the trusty M23 and subsequently its basically similar successor, the M26. But it took longer than expected developing the new car to a race-winning pitch, James's first triumph coming in the British Grand Prix at Silverstone. He was too far back to catch that consistent points earner Lauda

who recaptured his lost crown, although James also won the United States and Japanese races from the front.

Into 1978, McLaren began to slip from the competitive high wire. Slow off the mark in responding to the ground effect challenge posed by Lotus, the team suddenly found the M26 struggling hard to keep up. This downturn in performance adversely affected James's morale, even he admitting that he did not drive terribly well in the second half of the season.

At the end of the season he decided to leave, signing up with Walter Wolf's team for 1979 to drive a new ground effect car designed by Harvey Postlethwaite, the man who had produced the Hesketh machines in which James had made his name. But although the ability was quite clearly still there, Hunt's commitment had almost vanished.

He proved he could still run hard by hauling the Wolf up to fourth place before retiring from the Belgian Grand Prix, but by then he had concluded that the designer was more important than the driver in this era of under-car aerodynamics. After Monaco, James quit the cockpit and, unlike Alan Jones and Niki Lauda, he never came back.

job concealing the car's true secret from the opposition, attributing its outstanding performance to a preferential tank drainage system and rather special differential. The opposition seemed only too ready to accept this explanation, and Lotus was perfectly happy if they did.

Andretti's sensitive mechanical approach helped refine and develop the concept, the Italian-born American winning at Long Beach, Jarama, Dijon-Prenois and Monza, while his team-mate Gunnar Nilsson took the rain-soaked Belgian Grand Prix at Zolder after an over-impetuous first lap lunge on Mario's part produced immediate retirement after a collision with Watson's Brabham-Alfa Romeo.

Minor problems with the first Lotus 'wing car' included an aerodynamically cluttered rear end, with the airflow spilling out from beneath the two side pod venturis into a tangle of outboard mounted rear suspension components. Also, its centre of pressure (the point at which maximum downforce is generated) was slightly too far forward, offering better grip at the front end than at the rear. This was balanced by using slightly more downforce from the conventional rear wing than might have seemed ideal, the resultant drag slightly handicapping the 78 in terms of straight line speed. There was also an unfortunate spate of failures with the special development Nicholson-McLaren-prepared Cosworth DFV engines used by the team during that season.

All these lessons were learned for 1978 when Chapman further enhanced the concept to produce the beautiful full ground effect type 79, the car which produced that immortal quote from Andretti that 'if it hugged the road any closer, it would be white line. . . .'

With inboard suspension tucked in tightly front and rear, and a central single fuel cell that did not intrude into the crucial side

Above: Mario Andretti, possibly the most charismatic World Champion of all, won the title in 1978 for Lotus.

Left: Mario heading for the Lotus 79's maiden victory in the 1978 Belgian Grand Prix at Zolder.

Above right: Mario and Ronnie Peterson were close rivals and firm friends.

Right: Andretti and Peterson heading to their last 1-2 success with the Lotus 79 in the 1978 Dutch Grand Prix.

pod area, the Lotus 79 was a smooth, clean concept from the classically innovative Chapman mould. Andretti was now partnered by Ronnie Peterson, the former Lotus team star willingly accepting number two status in his quest for rejuvenation after a dismal patch with March and Tyrrell. Poor Nilsson had signed for Arrows, yet before the season started was stricken with terminal cancer and would not race again.

With cruel irony, the stricken Gunnar would survive to be present at Peterson's funeral. After a season which had seen Ronnie and Mario run riot across the Grand Prix stage, winning no fewer than eight races between them, Peterson sustained serious leg injuries in a multiple pile-up just after the start at Monza, a day that should have been joyous as Mario finally clinched his long sought-after World Championship.

Ronnie was badly hurt, but apparently not in immediate danger. Yet in one of those tragically rare developments, a bone marrow embolism entered his blood stream with fatal results. By Monday morning he was dead, and Andretti's delight was swamped in grief for the loss of a man whom he had come to regard as a highly principled friend.

The first Lotus 79 victory fell to Andretti on 21 May 1978, in the Belgian Grand Prix at Zolder. It seems hard to believe, but the last such success was in the Dutch Grand Prix on August 27 where Mario led Ronnie across the line for their fourth 1-2 finish of the year. Their reign of glory had lasted little barely over three months, for Andretti's Monza victory was wiped from the slate when a penalty was imposed for an over-eager start and they would not win again on the two race North American tour.

In 1979, the Lotus 79 would be dramatically eclipsed by its second-generation ground effect rivals. Yet Chapman's Black Beauties had a far-reaching impact on Grand Prix car design totally disproportionate to their fleeting summer in the F1 limelight.

Team-mates and friends

The pressures of driving with and competing against a team-mate frequently become a challenge so stifling for a Grand Prix driver that he is unable to sustain particularly cordial relations with his colleague. Yet there have been memorable exceptions to this rule, partnerships in which relations between the two drivers were founded on mutual respect and admiration, and which have blossomed into firm friendships when away from the circuit.

When Mario Andretti heard that Lotus veteran Ronnie Peterson was being re-hired for the 1978 Grand Prix season, he growled menacingly 'tell me where it's written that this team needs two number two drivers?' But in fact, Mario had unwittingly created the situation where Colin Chapman looked to Peterson as his team-mate for 1978, by asking for an increased retainer after discussing a deal with Ferrari when a preliminary agreement with Lotus had already been reached. Chapman could easily have refused Mario, pointing out that they already had a firm arrangement, but he knew racing drivers well enough to appreciate that keeping a star like Andretti in a sympathetic frame of mind would reap its own rewards.

So Chapman paid the extra, then accepted Peterson into the team on a sponsored basis. Ronnie was anxious to get a top-line drive after a couple of years in the wilderness and could provide additional sponsorship from a couple of sources which would help offset the extra Chapman had paid to Mario.

Andretti was initially extremely cautious about his arrangement, perhaps wondering whether Colin had sought to undermine his position. Yet Ronnie specifically accepted the role of number two. 'It is Mario's testing ability that has helped make the Lotus 79 the car it is,' Ronnie would remark later in the year, 'so it's only right that he should win the Championship.'

From some drivers, such remarks might have been construed as faintly patronising, but Ronnie spoke from the heart. He was genuinely grateful for the set of circumstances which enabled him to start rebuilding his reputation and, after the initial signs of tension evaporated, the two men got on superbly well.

Although Andretti benefitted on paper from the contractual stipulation that Peterson had to play second fiddle to him out on the circuit, the American driver had too much self-respect to cruise round at the front of the field, secure in the knowledge that the terms of his contract secured his position.

'I didn't want Ronnie to feel he was letting me win races,' Mario recalled over a decade later, 'so I ran as hard as I possibly could and he worked really hard to keep up in many places, of that I'm sure. Take the 1978 French Grand Prix at Paul Ricard as an example. I know a lot of people believed we were just cruising round ahead of Hunt, but that McLaren was chasing Ronnie really hard and I, in turn, was having to run my engine up against the rev. limiter to stay ahead of him on the straight. Hell, that was one flat-out motor race, whatever it may have looked like from outside.'

Mario, five years the senior driver, fully understood why Ronnie accepted an offer to drive for the McLaren team for 1979, appreciating that the Swede now felt his reputation was suffi-

Left: James Hunt (far left) in company with Mario Andretti and Ronnie Peterson.

Opposite page (clockwise from top left): Gilles Villeneuve and Jody Scheckter were neighbours in Monaco as well as Ferrari team-mates, but that did not prevent Gilles from beating his friend to win the 1979 South African Grand Prix, Jody's home race.

Left and below: Jody Scheckter and Gilles Villeneuve both won three races during 1979 with the square-cut Ferrari 312T4.

Right: Cosworth guiding light Keith Duckworth looks dubiously at the first Renault turbo V6.

Bottom right: Jean-Pierre Jabouille briefly shows the new French car's tail during a troubled debut in the 1977 British Grand Prix.

ciently reassembled to stand as a front-line number one driver in his own right. But he was absolutely heart-broken, thunderstruck, at Ronnie's sudden death in the wake of that terrible startline accident at Monza in 1978. 'He was the best team-mate I ever worked with, a really neat guy,' were the words Andretti regularly used to recall his friend and team-mate in the years to come.

Unlike the Andretti/Peterson partnership, the personal bond which built up between Jody Scheckter and Gilles Villeneuve in 1979 looked like being a far more serious affair from the outset. Villeneuve had been a member of the Maranello line-up for a year, and had already won his first Grand Prix, when the highly experienced Scheckter signed up at the start of the season. The seasoned South African driver had been one of F1's most spectacular new stars during the early years of the decade, producing some wild performances at the wheel of a McLaren M23. His extrovert antics included triggering the first lap multiple pile-up that destroyed half the field in the 1973 British Grand Prix, but he quickly settled down after joining Tyrrell at the start of '74.

By the end of '76, his partnership with Ken's team had run its course, so he switched to the newly refurbished Walter Wolf Racing team, winning three Grands Prix in 1977 to finish runner-up in the World Championship. In the summer of 1978, Jody had the opportunity of trying the new ground effect Wolf WR5 at Ferrari's Fiorano test track, and the Italian team carefully monitored his progress. They suddenly realised just how quick a driver Scheckter was and signed him up for the 1979 season.

Both Jody and Gilles faced the new year together aiming for the Championship, yet it says a lot for the former's maturity that he did not become downcast when Villeneuve won both the South African and Long Beach Grands Prix early in the season. 'I knew just how quick Gilles was,' reflected Jody, 'and although in terms of sheer speed, he was faster than me, I could recognise he was still prone to making the youthful errors just as I'd done in my early years. I figured that I would be the more consistent finisher . . .'

In fact, the two men had a well-matched season, winning three Grands Prix apiece. Yet Gilles faced the ultimate test of character when he found himself in the position at Monza when, running second behind Scheckter, he knew he only had to overtake his team-mate to become World Champion. Yet his principled nature obliged him to abide by the Ferrari convention in such circumstances, namely that whatever order the cars are

running in when they assume first and second place, that should remain unchanged all the way to the finish.

'I must admit that I just kept hoping that Jody's car would break down,' said Villeneuve afterwards, but he had self-belief not to let his own confidence be undermined by such an obvious disappointment.

Off-track, Villeneuve and Scheckter lived close to one another in Monaco, sharing each other's social life to a degree without living in each other's pockets. Jody thought Villeneuve was a hare-brained driver away from the circuit and, when word came from Maranello that they were both needed for a Fiorano test session, he always volunteered to drive on the four hour trip to Italy. Later, after Villeneuve acquired a helicopter, Jody refused to ride with him after one nerve-wracking flight in which a warning light on the instrument panel repeatedly kept flashing. Jody staggered away from the craft, calling Gilles a 'mad bastard' which almost certainly he was.

To see Jody and Gilles indulging in their lighthearted banter was to see two men whose friendship had grown to the point where they could indulge in fearful rows without either taking long-term offence. Theirs was a less formal relationship than Mario had with Ronnie, but, in both cases, there was no denying the air of mutual respect they each radiated for the other's ability behind the wheel of a Grand Prix car. Some partnerships which followed in the mid and late 1980s were to be characterised by no such good-natured candour.

Renault's Trend-setting Turbo

The 1977 British Grand Prix saw the French Renault company field the first contemporary turbocharged Grand Prix car, taking advantage of an unplugged hole in the technical regulations which was dated back to the end of the 1½-litre Formula 1 in 1965.

Concerned that there might be an insufficient number of competitors prepared to build full 3-litre engines for the new F1 regulations, the Comission Sportif Internationale (as the sport's governing body was then titled) produced what was later described as an equivalency formula by permitting the use of supercharged 1½-litre engines. More accurately, this should have been described as an 'expediency formula' designed to accommodate those who had in mind supercharging redundant 1½-litre Coventry Climax or BRM V8 engines to take part in the new category.

As things turned out, the new 3-litre naturally aspirated F1 was well enough supported for there to be no need for anybody to take advantage of these makeshift, interim provisions. But they lay dormant in the rule book for over ten years before Renault decided to capitalise on them with a 1½-litre V6 engine fitted with exhaust gas turbocharging to boost its power output.

Turbocharging is a means of using the exhaust gases to increase intake manifold pressure, a concept originally used to sustain manifold pressure on piston engined aeroplane engines. The higher the altitude, the thinner the air, so the more restricted an engine's breathing becomes, with consequent, obvious drop-off in power output. For racing applications, turbocharging offered the prospect of 'instant' extra power, although the strains and stresses imposed on those engines would require a great deal of mechanical ingenuity to surmount before the

turbocharged Grand Prix car reached its heyday in the mid-1980s.

The biggest advantage the turbo offered over the old-style mechanically driven supercharger was that virtually no mechanical demands were made on the engine itself in powering this additional source of power. The only real limiting factor was the back pressure against which the pistons had to battle on the exhaust stroke, although by ensuring that the boost pressure in the intake manifold equalled, or exceeded, the pressure in the exhaust manifold, that could be overcome. However, as Renault would soon discover, there were all manner of thermodynamic problems produced by the enormous heat build-up in a turbo-

Left and below: Jean-Pierre Jabouille's debut with the Renault RS1 turbo in the 1977 British Grand Prix was fleeting and ineffective.

Right and below right: Just two years later, the French turbo had been honed to a winning edge and Jabouille triumphed gloriously in the 1979 French Grand Prix at Dijon-Prenois.

charged F1 engine, not to mention the challenge of solving throt-tle response difficulties.

Seasoned F3, F2 and sports car campaigner Jean-Pierre Jabouille was assigned the task of handling the stubby Renault RS01 test bed for development and preliminary racing purposes throughout 1977, although the Renault Sport management made it quite clear that the F1 programme took second place for the time being. The clear number one priority was winning Le Mans with the team's 2-litre turbocharged sports cars, and when Jean-Pierre Jaussaud and Didier Pironi duly notched up that achievement in June 1978, the green light was given to con-centrate the racing team's efforts on the Grand Prix programme.

After an inauspicious debut in the '77 British Grand Prix, where Jabouille retired with a split exhaust system and con-sequent loss of turbo boost pressure, the French team ran an intermittent programme of races for the balance of the season as it came to grips with its technical challenge. But in 1978, Jabouille ran a full season in the flat-bottomed type RS01, scor-ing the marque's first Championship points with a fourth place finish in the United States Grand Prix at Watkins Glen.

Suitably encouraged, René Arnoux was recruited as second driver for the 1979 season and when Jabouille qualified on pole position for the South African Grand Prix at Kyalami, the track near Johannesburg situated some 5000ft above sea level, the benefits of turbos pitted against naturally aspirated engines at high altitude were graphically illustrated.

One of the earliest problems encountered by Renault was that of 'turbo lag'; namely, that when the driver took his foot off the throttle, so the compressor turbines slowed down and, when the throttle was opened again, there was a perceptible gap before boost pressure built up again. This might be all very well for a commercial vehicle diesel engine, but it was not acceptable in a Formula 1 environment.

Renault engine specialist Bernard Dudot sought to tackle this problem by replacing the single larger Garrett turbo fitted to the V6 by a pair of smaller KKK turbos, each serving one bank of the V6 cylinder engine, in time for the 1979 Monaco Grand Prix. This twin turbocharged engine also employed a water intercooler to reduce the temperature of the air entering the engine, this development considerably enhancing the life of the hard-worked V6 engine's pistons.

This revised engine was packaged in a brand new chassis which exploited ground effect aerodynamics to the maximum and, when Jabouille won the French Grand Prix at Dijon-Prenois, Arnoux finishing third behind Villeneuve's Ferrari 312T5, Renault had scored the first victory to herald an avalanche of turbo success that would follow in the 1980s.

Renault itself would win many more Grands Prix, but never a World Championship, and was eventually eclipsed in the turbo race by the likes of Ferrari, TAG/Porsche and Honda. Yet the French team had been the pioneers in a revolution which would dramatically raise the Formula 1 technical stakes, changing the whole emphasis of Grand Prix racing in a manner which would far outlast the turbos into the new era of 3.5-litre naturally aspirated engines in 1989.

Left: Jabouille beat Villeneuve's Ferrari 312T4 and the second Renault turbo of his more youthful team-mate Rene Arnoux with a fine performance in front of his home crowd at Dijon in 1979.

Above: Jabouille on the rostrum with Arnoux (left).

Centre right: Ayrton Senna used Renault power in his Lotus to great effect in 1985 and 86.

Right: The Ligier team used Renault turbo power between 1984 and 87. This is Philippe Streiff in the 1985 Grand Prix of Europe at Brands Hatch.

Frank Makes the Big Time

When Clay Regazzoni won the 1979 British Grand Prix at Silverstone at the wheel of the Saudia Williams FW07, ten years had elapsed since the late Piers Courage finished fifth in the same event driving a private Brabham BT26 entered by Frank Williams Racing Cars. In the decade separating those two events, Britain's most ambitious and determined team owner since Colin Chapman had fought tenaciously for his very existence before finally establishing an enduring foundation for his Grand Prix efforts.

Frank Williams tried his hand behind the wheel during the early 1960s, but his exploits first with an Austin A40 and later with an F3 Cooper served to convince him that he himself was probably not World Championship material. So he set himself up in business dealing in second-hand racing cars, running a spares and preparation service, before finally entering the F2 arena in 1968 with a Brabham BT23C driven by Piers Courage, the heir to the British brewing dynasty of the same name.

Suitably encouraged by Piers' progress, Williams managed to negotiate the purchase of an F1 Brabham for 1969, although this had to be done via a third party as the works Brabham team had a Goodyear tyre contract and Frank's cars were tied to running on Dunlops. Courage, who had displayed more of that quality than was prudent during his formative years in motor racing, now matured into a forceful and respected performer, producing second places in the 1969 Monaco and United States Grands Prix, actually beating Brabham's works car after a splendid battle in the latter event.

Suitably encouraged by his fledgling team's performance, Williams took another giant step for 1970, coming to an agreement with Italian constructor Alessandro de Tomaso for the manufacture of a purpose-built F1 chassis for Piers' exclusive use. Just as this new project began to show signs of making the grade, Courage was killed in a fiery crash during the Dutch Grand Prix at Zandvoort, effectively wiping out Frank's F1 effort as well as leaving him deeply saddened at the loss of a close friend.

De Tomaso was understandably demoralised by the tragedy, and while Frank struggled through the balance of the season with Australian new boy Tim Schenken driving, the Italian constructor did not continue the arrangement in 1971. That left Williams seeking to rebuild his entire operation from scratch, a task he tackled with his usual irrepressible zeal. Buying an 'off-the-peg' March 711, he gathered together sufficient sponsorship from Palitoys, the Italian model car makers, to run Frenchman Henri Pescarolo, a steady, unspectacular performer, and was rewarded with a fourth place at Silverstone.

For 1972, Frank continued running March machinery, although the questionable durability of the original product led the Williams team progressively to rebuild the cars round its own strengthened monocoques as the season progressed. Expanding his operation to run a second car for promising young Brazilian Carlos Pace, Frank actually produced his own chassis, dubbed the Palitoys, but Pescarolo crashed it early on in the British Grand Prix.

Above: Alan Jones, seen here winning the 1979 German Grand Prix, drove the superb Williams FW07 to win the 1980 Drivers' Cahmpionship.

Right: But it was Clay Regazzoni who finally nailed Frank's first victory in the 1979 British Grand Prix at Silverstone.

Left: Jacques Laffite's plodding Williams FW04 survived to second place in the 1975 German Grand Prix, just keeping the financially strapped team on the road.

It was subsequently revamped for 1973 when Frank seemed to have made the big time with sponsorship deals from Marlboro cigarettes and a link with the Iso-Rivolta sports car company. The cars were now entered as 'Iso-Marlboros', but no amount of name changing could rid Frank of an enduring problem, namely the need to pay last year's debts with next season's sponsorship money.

This sort of financial juggling was hardly conducive to fielding a competitive F1 challenge, but Frank struggled on through 1974 and 75, recruiting young Frenchman Jacques Laffite along the way. Things were really bad in '75, only Laffite's dogged slog to second place in the '75 German Grand Prix at Nurburgring keeping the team's head above water. But Frank knew he was in a parlous financial situation and had no real choice but to sell out to Austro-Canadian oil man Walter Wolf at the end of 1975.

Part of the deal was that Frank should stay on as an integral part of the team, but it soon became clear to him that his role was degenerating into that of Wolf's highly paid personal assistant. When he found himself being sent to collect his employer's new Mercedes from the factory during a Grand Prix weekend, Frank realised that this wasn't for him. Anyway, the Wolf team's programme, based round the development of the ambitious rubber-suspended Hesketh 308E, acquired when his Lordship's team closed its doors at the end of 1975, was floundering uncompetitively.

For all his disappointment over the years, Frank still wanted to go racing on his own account. He left Wolf Racing, together with junior engineer Patrick Head, and the two men set up business in a small way together. The 1977 British Grand Prix saw Williams returning to the scene as an entrant running a private March 761 for young Belgian novice Patrick Neve. The tiny team produced little in the way of results that year, but 1978 would see the newly formed Williams Grand Prix Engineering start out on the road to the top.

In a small factory close to Didcot railway station, Patrick Head produced the neat, compact Williams FW06. With Alan Jones signed to drive and, more crucially, sponsorship from Saudia airlines, the team made steady progress throughout a 1978 season dominated by the super ground effect Lotus 79s. The high spot was Jones's superb second place to Reutemann's Ferrari at Watkins Glen and, with Patrick Head developing his own ground-effect challenger for 1979, prospects at last looked excellent for Frank Williams and his colleagues.

The Williams FW07 was to take ground effect engineering into a second generation, its chassis being significantly stiffer than the Lotus 79's and therefore able to generate increased downforce more predictably. It did not make its race debut until the fifth round of the '79 Championship battle, but Jones and team-mate Clay Regazzoni quickly indicated that it was a highly competitive proposition. Pre-race testing at Silverstone revealed that, come the British Grand Prix, Jones would be the man to beat.

Left: Alan Jones heads his FW07B towards victory place in the 1980 Canadian Grand Prix.

Right: The talented, enigmatic Carlos Reutemann in the process of winning the 1980 Monaco Grand Prix for Frank.

Below: A dynamic partnership. Left to right, Patrick Head, Alan Jones and Frank Williams.

So it proved. After an initial skirmish with Jean-Pierre Jabouille's Renault turbo, Jones stormed off into the distance. Yet a cracked water pump, and consequent terminal overheating, denied the rugged Australian the privilege of notching up Frank's first Grand Prix win. As he rolled into the pit lane in a cloud of steam, Regazzoni went through into the lead and stayed there all the way to the chequered flag.

A decade of singleminded effort had at last been rewarded, unlocking an avalanche of success for Williams and his team in the years that followed. Jones would win four more races in 1979 before speeding to the 1980 World Championship with five victories. Carlos Reutemann would spend two years with the team (1980 and 81), winning three races, while Keke Rosberg picked up the gauntlet after Jones' retirement to take the Drivers' Championship in 1982.

The Williams team would remain in the forefront of the Grand Prix action throughout the 1980s, a vivid and enduring testimony to one man's determination to make his dreams come true in the sport's most exalted category.

Brabham Ups and Downs

At the end of 1969, Jack Brabham signalled his intention to retire from the cockpit by selling his shares in Motor Racing Developments to his long-time partner and confederate Ron Tauranac. Even though the three-times World Champion raced on for one final F1 season in 1970, during that final year he was, in effect, simply a 'hired hand' of the team he had helped to found almost a decade earlier.

At 44 years old, Jack was still sufficiently motivated to win the South African Grand Prix at Kyalami with the Cosworth-engined BT33 and had Rindt's Lotus 72 beaten in the British Grand Prix at Brands Hatch, the Austrian only sweeping by when Jack's engine spluttered out of fuel on the very last lap. Tauranac then faced the 1971 season with veteran Graham Hill and new boy Tim Schenken, the best result being the former's win in the Silverstone International Trophy meeting.

At around the time of the Monaco Grand Prix, Tauranac began talking with Bernie Ecclestone about the possibilities of selling at least a portion of the company to him. Grand Prix racing was moving into a highly commercial age and Ron admitted he was finding the financial side pretty daunting. Eventually a deal was done to sell the whole company to Ecclestone by the start of 1972, after which Tauranac briefly stayed on to superintend the design side before leaving to set up his own Ralt company, specialising in the manufacture of proprietary racing cars in the junior formulae.

Ecclestone himself had raced extensively in the late 1940s and early 1950s, but it was in the role of manager to the late Stuart Lewis-Evans that he established himself on the motor racing scene. In 1957, when Connaught Engineering withdrew from F1, Bernie acquired two of the cars and entered them for Lewis-Evans and Ivor Bueb in the Tasman series.

However, after Stuart died from injuries sustained when his Vanwall crashed in the 1958 Morroccan Grand Prix at Casablanca, Ecclestone dropped from the motor racing scene. He would return as Jochen Rindt's commercial manager in the late 1960s. Away from the track he was an astute and successful businessman with lucrative interests in several fields.

Ecclestone would soon establish himself as Grand Prix racing's most imaginative visionary, transforming the Formula One Constructors' Association into the most powerful lobby in the sport. He could also see the potential for Formula 1 to become one of the richest, most widely publicised sports in the world and set about achieving that aim as well as moulding the Brabham team into a consistently competitive fighting force.

Below left: Jack Brabham heads to victory with the Repco-engined BT19 in the 1966 French Grand Prix at Reims.

Right: Carlos Reutemann won the 1975 German Grand Prix with the elegant Gordon Murray-designed Brabham BT44B.

Below: Jack Brabham at the wheel of the Cosworth-engined BT33, leading at Monaco in 1970 prior to a last corner error which handed victory to Jochen Rindt's Lotus 49C.

Left: Bernie Ecclestone acquired control of the Brabham team in 1972, the first step to becoming the most powerful figure in Formula 1.

Below: Gordon Murray's pyramidal monocoque design, seen here on the BT44B, became his signature on most Brabham designs from the 1973 to 78 seasons.

Right: Although Graham Hill did not sign for Brabham until 1971, he tried this BT26 in practice for the 1969 British Grand Prix. Crouching alongside the car are (left) designer Ron Tauranac and (right) mechanic Ron Dennis, today boss of McLaren International.

Bernie's first full season in charge, 1972, was a patchy year of consolidation. Graham Hill stayed aboard, but now partnered by the very promising Argentinian Carlos Reutemann and Wilson Fittipaldi, elder brother of Lotus star Emerson. At the wheel of the distinctive 'lobster claw' Brabham BT34, Reutemann won the non-Championship Brazilian Grand Prix at Interlagos to set the tone of his future relationship with the team. Meanwhile, on the design side, Ecclestone gave a free hand to the lanky, South African-born Gordon Murray, the man who would be responsible for all the F1 Brabhams for the next fifteen years.

In 1973, Murray produced the first of his distinctive 'pyramid' monocoque machines, the BT42. Reutemann and Fittipaldi Snr. demonstrated its potential, but it was not until its successor, the BT44, came on the scene in 1974 that Reutemann established himself as a Grand Prix winner. The dusky South American won the South African, Austrian and United States Grands Prix in storming style. By the end of the season he was partnered by Brazil's Jose Carlos Pace, a contemporary of Emerson Fittipaldi and a significant rising star in his own right.

In 1975, Brabham benefitted from Martini sponsorship and Pace beat Fittipaldi's McLaren to a memorable victory in Brazil. Reutemann's tally amounted to a single lucky victory in the German Grand Prix, it now being evident that Ferrari's flat-12 engine was producing significantly more power than the Cosworth DFV, so Bernie set about securing Brabham its own exclusive source of engines for 1976. He forged a deal with Alfa Romeo for the use of the Italian company's flat-12 engine which had previously been used in their 33TT12 sports cars which won the 1975 World Manufacturer's Championship, admittedly against makeweight opposition. With a claimed power output of 510bhp at 12,000rpm at a time when a good Cosworth DFV developed 465bhp and even the arch-rival Ferrari flat-12 'only' 500 bhp, it certainly appeared a tantalizing prospect.

It was, however, an extremely thirsty and heavy engine and, while Murray worked hard to package it into the new BT45 chassis, Reutemann quickly lost interest after his first test in the new machine. The team was largely carried through 1973 by Pace's enthusiasm, Reutemann buying off the balance of his contract with the team in order to join Ferrari. Throughout the season he maintained that Ecclestone had misled him about Brabham's plans for 1976, Carlos labouring under the impression that a Cosworth-engined car would be taken to the South American races for purposes of evaluation against the Alfa machine. When that failed to happen, Reutemann's disillusionment was complete.

Beyond doubt, those early Alfa-engined cars were dreadfully unreliable and, in particular, suffered horrendous problems with the weight-saving carbon fibre brakes during the course of the year.

Nevertheless, the team had made considerable progress by the start of 1977 when John Watson joined up as Pace's teammate. The season started moderately well with Pace an encouraging second in Argentina as well as leading the first lap of the Brazilian Grand Prix. Tragically, the charismatic Brazilian was killed in a light aircraft crash a few weeks prior to the European season, bequeathing team leadership to Watson.

Left: Niki Lauda won the 1978 Italian Grand Prix at Monza with the Alfa flat-12 powered BT46 only after Mario Andretti and Gilles Villeneuve were penalised.

Below left: Lauda struggles with the strangulated Alfa V12-powered BT48 in the 1979 Spanish Grand Prix at Jarama.

Right: Nelson Piquet won the 1981 Argentine Grand Prix using a highly controversial suspension lowering system on his Brabham BT49C.

Below: Gordon Murray's capacity for innovation was working overtime with the BT46 'fan car' which Lauda used to win the 1978 Swedish Grand Prix.

The Ulsterman drove splendidly for much of the year in the purposeful Brabham BT45B, looking set for victory in the French Grand Prix until fuel feed problems intervened, allowing Mario Andretti's Lotus 78 to slip by to win in a last lap re-run of events at Brands Hatch seven years earlier. The BT45Bs finished the 1977 season without a single victory, but Murray was encouraged by their form and embarked on a radical new chassis design in 1978.

Taking a close look at the Alfa engine set up yet again, he decided that he could in fact package the necessary fuel load into his favourite pyramidal chassis configuration. But he also decided to adopt the very advanced concept of surface cooling, recessing heat exchangers for the water and oil systems into both sides of the monocoque surface.

Unfortunately, the system was fraught with problems and quite simply did not work, the prototype overheating dramatically during a test at Donington Park in mid winter. It was not even worth thinking what might happen in the broiling heat of Buenos Aires.

The BT46s were quickly rebuilt with conventional front-mounted water radiators for Watson and new recruit Niki Lauda to drive, but the challenge posed by the ground effect Lotus 79s posed Murray an even bigger headache once the '78 season got underway. The flat-12 engine precluded the use of underbody venturis, so Murray came up with the novel 'fan car' concept, whereby a giant gearbox driven fan was fitted to the rear of the BT46, sucking out the air from beneath the skirted-off underside of the car and thus producing prodigious downforce.

Lauda used the fan car to splendid effect, winning the Swedish Grand Prix at Anderstorp to a chorus of disapproval from rival teams who believed that such a concept breached the regulations relating to aerodynamic devices. There followed an esoteric debate as to whether the fan's primary purpose was to create downforce or cool the engine, but Ecclestone wisely chose not to risk a rift in FOCA solidarity and withdrew the car from any further races.

In an attempt to provide Gordon Murray with the equipment to produce a definitive ground-effect car, Alfa Romeo re-vamped the flat-12 into a 60-degree V12 in time for the 1979 season, but the new engine again proved disastrously unreliable. By the end of the 1979 season, Brabham had switched back to the Cosworth engine and, while Niki Lauda had suddenly made the decision to retire from the sport mid-way through practice in Canada, his newly recruited team-mate Nelson Piquet was already establishing quite a reputation as one to watch. He would sustain that reputation to considerable effect as Grand Prix racing moved into the 1980s.

Bernie and Balestre –
The Battle for Control in F1

Between 1979 and 83 an amazingly intense and hostile confrontation between the two strongest bodies involved in Grand Prix racing threatened to tear the sport asunder. In opposing corners were the supposed forces of law, order and administration, in the form of the sport's governing body, and the powerful Formula One Constructors' Association under the dynamic leadership of Bernard Ecclestone.

As FOCA grew in strength and influence throughout much of the 1970s, its obvious rise to prominence was largely ignored by the sport's governing body, the Commission Sportive Internationale (CSI) which later changed its title to the Federation Internationale de Sport Automobile (FISA). During that time FOCA became the power base of Grand Prix racing. If you wanted to stage a race, you spoke to Ecclestone; if you wanted to enter F1 with a team, you spoke to Ecclestone. The Brabham team owner organised start money packages and secured television coverage. Organisers did not pay out on a published prize scale, they handed the whole amount over to FOCA which then distributed among its members by means of a complex formula.

It had almost got to the point where FISA was effectively bypassed as a meaningful organisation. True, for legal and administrative purposes, it sanctioned the races, but its authority had become somewhat theoretical by the time Jean-Marie Balestre became elected to the FISA Presidency at the end of 1978.

Suddenly, FOCA's comfy ride seemed to be over. An extrovert, theatrical, stubborn and massively determined man, Balestre set out on a crusade to restore FISA's sporting power and reduce the influence of the constructors. Much to the irritation of the men who invested the money to field the cars, Balestre would develop a worryingly impulsive approach to administering the sport at its most exalted level, tending to shoot from the hip first and ask questions afterwards.

At the 1979 Argentine Grand Prix, first race of the season, John Watson's McLaren became involved in a first corner tangle with Jody Scheckter's McLaren. The race was flagged to a halt and Balestre leaped in with both feet; to this day, Watson believes that he had a strong influence on the steward's decision to impose a draconian fine on the McLaren driver.

Left: Bernie Ecclestone built the Formula One Constructors' Association into the most powerful commercial force within Grand Prix racing during the 1970s and 80s.

Right: Ecclestone knew precisely who it was necessary to court. Here he is chatting with Lee Gaug, Goodyear's streetwise and highly respected international racing manager. Goodyear withdrew briefly in 1981, sick of the bickering between FISA and FOCA.

In 1980, Balestre's regime at FISA would announce a ban, nominally on safety grounds, on the sliding skirt systems which were such a fundamental element behind the competitiveness of the ground effect era. With Renault's star in the ascendant, FOCA saw this as the French governing body favouring the French national team. They determined to fight it and, as a result, a confrontation was engineered.

Early in the year, it was made clear by FISA that any driver failing to attend the official pre-race briefing would be fined. At Zolder and Monaco, several teams encouraged their men not to bother turning up. Suddenly, a crisis arose. Balestre said that the culprits would be suspended. FOCA accused FISA of being deliberately provocative and demanded that the fines be rescinded.

This whole affair came to a head with a sanctioning dispute over the Spanish Grand Prix at Jarama. FISA and FOCA put forward lengthy arguments to support their case. In the event, the race went ahead, but without Ferrari, Renault or Alfa Romeo, all of whom had interests in Motorsport outside the F1 arena and, on balance, found it impossible to support a pirate race. The race went ahead, was won by Alan Jones's Williams – and was not allowed to count for the Championship.

One up to FISA. But FOCA would live to fight again, laying plans for its own independent World Federation of Motor Sports which, said Ecclestone, would run an alternative World Championship for sliding skirt cars in 1981. It was an impossible situation; FISA had the authority and influence over the circuits, but FOCA had the vast majority of the cars. Neither could exist without the other.

FISA insisted that fixed side skirts be introduced for 1981, but FOCA went ahead with its own pirate race in South Africa under the old sliding skirt rules. Won by Carlos Reutemann's Williams, again it was deemed inadmissible as a World Championship qualifying round. Eventually, just prior to the Long Beach Grand Prix, FISA and FOCA reached a rapprochement. An armistice was arrived at with the signing of the Concorde Agreement, a wide-ranging document which laid out the procedures whereby regulations could be changed and, while acknowledging FISA's role as the sporting power, effectively left the financial control in the hands of the Constructors.

The peace, such as it was, proved extremely fragile. At the start of 1982, controversy erupted again when the lighter Cosworth-engined cars began using replenishable brake cooling reservoirs as a means to run under-weight during the race. This was prohibited in one of FISA's familiar 'rule clarifications', a means by which the governing body sought to tinker with the regulations from time to time without going through their own proper procedures. FOCA then boycotted the San Marino Grand Prix at Imola, leaving Ferrari and Renault to entertain the crowds on their own, a task which they managed admirably.

At the end of 1982, FISA suddenly announced that under-car aerodynamics would be severely restricted for the following season, requiring all F1 cars to have flat undersides. This was imposed under the proviso which enabled the usual two-year notice period for technical rule changes to be by-passed if the matter was regarded as one affecting car or circuit safety.

Far from becoming easier with the passing of the years, the atmosphere of tension and uncertainty between Balestre and the F1 Constructors would last throughout the 1980s, culminating in the massive legal dispute between FISA and the McLaren team over the question of Ayrton Senna's disqualification from the 1989 Japanese Grand Prix. Yet, by then, Balestre would have been re-elected unanimously to the FISA Presidency for the fifth consecutive time. It looked as though the only way of deposing him would be to put up a rival candidate for the job who might have a hope of beating him, a challenge which almost seemed less likely in 1990 than it had been ten years earlier.

Left: Derek Daly's Tyrell was launched into orbit over team-mate Jean-Pierre Jarier on the first corner of the 1980 Monaco Grand Prix, but nobody was hurt thanks to fast-improving standards of car construction and circuit safety.

Below left: The same happy outcome attaches to this spectacular collision between Piquet's Brabham and Patrese's Alfa Romeo at Monaco five years later.

Right: Familiar sight in pit lanes all over the world – Bernie Ecclestone (*right*) and Jean-Marie Balestre in conference together.

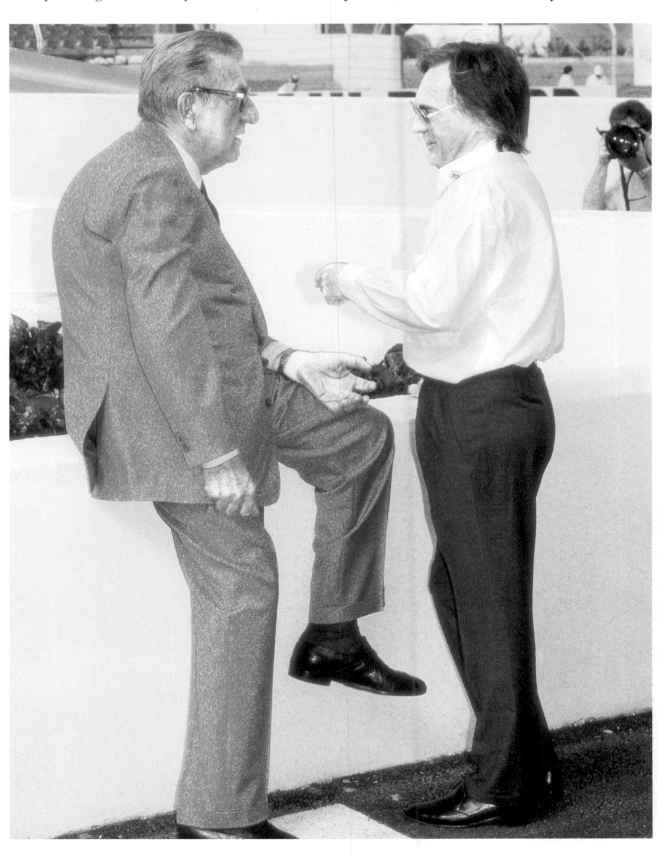

Part 5

The Modern Era

Villeneuve, Prost and Senna

Several drivers played out pivotal roles during the late 1970s and early 80s, so selecting a handful to put under the microscope for more detailed analysis could be interpreted as unfair to those who were left out. The best reference point we have is probably provided by Patrick Tambay, the genial Frenchman who won a couple of Grands Prix for Ferrari in the wake of Villeneuve's death and Pironi's debilitating practice accident at Hockenheim in 1982.

'In my time, the three drivers I saw racing with that extra something, the quality setting them apart from their rivals, were Villeneuve, Prost and Senna,' insists Tambay. The three men provide a fascinating cross-section of the talent and temperament required to perform as a top line Formula 1 driver, in many ways so different, in some respects very similar. Bound together by the same overwhelming will and determination to excel at their chosen sport, if you met them socially you would have found it difficult to believe they were members of the same profession.

Villeneuve was fearless, cheerful and extrovert. To this pint-sized French Canadian, life was for living and Grand Prix racing was the stage on which he played. Absolutely confident in his own ability, he was a man of honour who judged his own personal success by the number of races he won. World Championships were important, he conceded, but winning races was what the business was all about.

Married and a father of two young children by the time he was recruited by Ferrari at the end of 1977, Villeneuve had honed his fearlessness to a fine edge. A regular competitor in snowmobile races since he was a teenager, he had climbed the motor racing ladder through Formula Ford into the Canadian domestic Formula Atlantic category, shooting to prominence in a wider arena by beating Alan Jones and James Hunt in the 1976 Trois Rivières street race.

Gilles had a straightforward and uncomplicated approach to his motor racing which struck an affectionate chord with the oft-autocratic Enzo Ferrari. His lack of complexity reminded the Commendatore of his salad days when racers were just that, not highly-paid businessmen who arrived at his factory in grey suits to negotiate their contracts.

His critics say he over-drove dramatically, an argument which conveniently forgets that he seldom drove cars which handled as well as the opposition. His first victory came in the '78 Canadian Grand Prix at Montreal with the Ferrari 312T3, his last in the '81 Spanish race in the turbo 126CK. He died in practice for the 1982 Belgian Grand Prix, battling to lap faster than team-mate Didier Pironi, the man who had double-crossed him a fortnight earlier and won the San Marino Grand Prix against established team orders.

Villeneuve's relaxed familiarity was a trait that seemed alien to Ayrton Senna, although the Brazilian's flair behind the wheel

Previous page: Nigel Mansell's Lotus 95T Renault led the rain-soaked 1984 Monaco Grand Prix before the English driver spun off and damaged the car.

Left: Villeneuve's Ferrari doggedly pursues Jones' Williams during their epic battle for victory in the 1979 Canadian Grand Prix, won by Jones.

Above: Gilles' Ferrari 312T4 briefly ahead of Jones in the early stages of the race.

Right: Didier Pironi (28) and Villeneuve in close contention at Imola in 1982, Villeneuve's last Grand Prix before his fatal accident.

Left: Ayrton Senna splashes to victory in the 1988 British Grand Prix at Silverstone in the McLaren-Honda MP4/4.

Right: Prost shadows team-mate Niki Lauda, both in McLaren-TAGs, during their spectacular 1984 season when they won 12 out of 16 races.

Below right: Prost explains why he is quitting McLaren, summer, 1989.

Below: Prost celebrates his victory in the 1987 Portuguese Grand prix, a success which beat Jackie Stewart's long-standing record of 27 career victories.

was every bit as natural and raw as the Canadian's. They never raced together. Gilles had been dead almost two years when Ayrton burst on the F1 scene at the start of 1984 at the wheel of a Toleman-Hart. From the outset, it was clear that this courteous, formally distant young man from Sao Paolo was something quite out of the ordinary.

His sensational run to second place behind Prost's McLaren at Monaco in torrential rain suggested that Senna's talent had already outstripped the technical potential of the Toleman team. Sure enough, he switched to Team Lotus at the end of the year, and scored its first win since the death of Colin Chapman two and a half years before with a brilliant performance in monsoon conditions at Estoril, when driving the Renault-engined Type 95T.

He stayed with Team Lotus for three seasons, raising morale and making himself tremendously popular. 'When you worked with Ayrton, you knew he was giving his total effort,' remembers one of the mechanics. 'If a driver repays your effort like that, the people who work with him respond very enthusiastically.' With Renault power through to the end of '86, then a year with Honda's V6, Senna imbued Lotus with hope and motivation. Technically, though, the team was unable to deliver a World Championship-winning chassis, so Ayrton switched to McLaren for 1988.

Alongside the gregarious Prost, this ascetic Brazilian may not have turned himself into the media's favourite man, but that is not a prime consideration for Senna. He applies more concentrated energy to the business of being the best Grand Prix driver than any of his contemporaries; all extraneous elements are ruthlessly eliminated from his mind while he sifts, analyses and ponders. The result at the end of the Grand Prix weekend may

not always be what Senna sought, but you can always rely on him to give every race his best shot.

On track, Senna's ruthless unwillingness to compromise has got him into quite a few scrapes, many with the similarly motivated Nigel Mansell. In that respect, he is the absolute antithesis of the man who was his McLaren team-mate in 1988 and 89. Alain Prost's record Formula 1 success in achieving 39 career victories has been achieved by a combination of stealth, judgement, mechanical sympathy and the ability to be outstandingly quick when the need arises.

Prost's critics regard him as a highly political animal, an interesting observation in itself. If true, then Prost is a most accomplished performer, widely regarded as the most genuine and uncomplicated of current F1 drivers. While Senna wins, indeed seeks to dominate, by drawing enormously on his emotional and mental reserves, Prost has survived for a decade as a front-line F1 driver by conserving his resources, drawing on them sparingly. Knowing that races and Championships fall not always to the fastest, he came to understand that keeping out of trouble is the number one priority.

Prost's first victory, the 1981 French Grand Prix, came at the wheel of a Renault in only his second year of F1. Since then, he has won a minimum of two races each season. In total, he achieved nine victories for Renault and followed them up with a further thirty wins for McLaren, as well as World Championship titles in 1985 and 86.

Prost's critics should ponder one significant fact; you do not win 39 Grand Prix races by accident. For 1990, Alain joined Nigel Mansell at Ferrari. It would be a brave man who bet against the Frenchman winning a few more races before he finally called it a day.

The Rise and Rise of McLaren International

Bruce McLaren's name has been linked with Formula 1 racing for over thirty years, the shy New Zealander making his debut at the wheel of an F2 Cooper-Climax in the 1958 German Grand Prix. In the early 1960s he would establish a polished reputation as a Grand Prix driver, not quite in the front rank, and later gained fame for establishing his own team to contest not only the World Championship, but also the financially lucrative North American Can-Am series for big-engined sports cars.

It was while testing one of his own Can-Am McLarens at Goodwood in June 1970, that Bruce McLaren met his death, but his name has lived on and is currently synonymous with the highest possible standards of Grand Prix technology and engineering. Although only formally established in 1980, McLaren International, now part of the TAG/McLaren group, has fielded the World Champion's car in 1984, 85, 86, 88 and 89. Prior to the start of the 1990 season, McLaren stands second only to Ferrari in the all-time Grand Prix winners' stakes.

Bruce McLaren himself won the marque's first Grand prix victory in 1968, nipping through to take his Cosworth-engined M7 to victory at Spa-Francorchamps after Jackie Stewart's hitherto-dominant Matra MS10 ran short of fuel in the closing stages. After his death, the team would continue in the same highly professional vein, the majority shareholder now being Teddy Mayer. An American former tax lawyer, Teddy had first become involved in racing through his brother Tim, a promising young rising star who was killed driving a McLaren team Cooper-Climax in the Tasman formula race at Longford, Tasmania, at the start of 1964.

Having recovered from this tragedy, Teddy decided to continue his involvement with motorsport and became one of the four founding directors of the McLaren company, along with

Bruce, Tyler Alexander (Tim Mayer's one-time mechanic) and Jack Brabham's former business manager Phil Kerr. The three surviving partners would keep the show firmly on the road throughout the first half of the 1970s.

The success of the Gordon Coppuck-designed McLaren M23, and its closely related successor the M26, kept McLaren winning all the way through to 1977. They won World Championship titles in 1974 (Emerson Fittipaldi) and 1976 (James Hunt), but the period 1978-80 saw the team in decline. It misjudged both the significance and intensity of the ground effect revo-

Above: From left to right, Niki Lauda, Ron Dennis, engineer Alan Jenkins and Alain Prost share an amusing moment during the 1984 season.

Left: Prost, Senna and the entire team celebrate the McLaren-Honda domination of 1988 with a team photograph.

Top right: Ron Dennis was the architect and motivating force behind McLaren International.

Right: John Watson's victory in the 1981 British Grand Prix at Silverstone was the first of many.

lution and was late exploiting the advantages of under-car aero-dynamics. Moreover, when Coppuck did so, with the gargantuan McLaren M28, it was slow and unsuccessful. As a panic measure, the team rushed through the new M29 in time for the '79 British Grand Prix at Silverstone and, while it was definitely an improvement, it was no Williams FW07, the machine that McLaren had sought to mimic.

At the same time that McLaren fortunes were tumbling down-hill, Formula 2 team owner Ron Dennis was actively contem-plating a move up into F1. His enthusiasm for motor racing stemming more from a regard for technical excellence rather than any fundamental love of cars, Dennis had arrived on the Grand Prix scene in 1967 as a twenty year old junior mechanic working on Jochen Rindt's Cooper-Maserati. He later moved on to become chief mechanic of the Brabham team before estab-lishing his own F2 team, Rondel Racing, with a couple of hired Brabham-Cosworths at the start of 1970.

Rondel Racing brought fresh standards of professionalism and careful turn-out to this highly competitive international formula. They planned an F1 car for 1974, but the economic down-turn caused by the famous fuel crisis caused the plans to be shelved and Rondel simply ceased trading. Ron would con-tinue operating throughout the 1970s with a succession of well-run F2 programmes and, in 1979, also fielded Niki Lauda's BMW M1 in the highly promoted 'Procar' series of races which supported many of the European Grands Prix.

Late in 1979 he made contact with former Chaparral Indy car designer John Barnard who had been recommended to him by Frank Williams' chief designer Patrick Head. Barnard, who had served his motor racing apprenticeship in the early 1970s along-side Head at Lola Cars, the Huntingdon-based manufacturers of production racing cars, thought Dennis was looking for some-

Left: Watson drove smoothly and consistently at Silverstone to bag that 1981 victory.

Below: Lauda has just slipped past de Cesaris' Alfa to take the lead of the 1982 US Grand Prix West at Long Beach, his first win following his return from retirement.

Right: The McLaren team assemble for the photographer before the 1984 Portuguese Grand Prix.

Below right: Lauda en route to victory at Long Beach, 1982. He was second to team-mate John Watson the following year.

body to design him an F2 car. Only when they met did Barnard realise that Ron had F1 in mind, a happy meeting of minds, as it turned out, for John had some ambitious ideas on that front himself. He believed that it would be possible to manufacture an extremely light and very strong chassis from carbon fibre, then regarded as an extremely esoteric material, the use of which had been confined to the aerospace industry.

As Dennis worked out what sort of budget and engineering commitment might be involved in launching an F1 assault, McLaren's deteriorating form had increasingly become a matter of concern for the team's long-standing sponsors, Marlboro, whose colours had been on the cars since the start of 1974. In an effort to revitalise the prospects for its prime F1 operation, Marlboro engineered an amalgamation between McLaren and Ron Dennis's Project 4 organisation and a new company, McLaren International, came into being in September 1980.

Mayer's 85 per cent stake in the original Team McLaren now became a 45 per cent shareholding in McLaren International, which kept him as the biggest single shareholder. But the energy of Ron Dennis and his Project 4 partner Creighton Brown began to stamp its own distinctive identity on the team.

Dennis and Barnard successfully forged a deal with the Salt Lake City-based Hercules Aerospace organisation for the supply of the carbon fibre composite panels which would be bonded together to form the chassis of the radical new McLaren MP4. Aerodynamically smooth and sleek, with beautifully crafted detail finish and tight-fitting body panels, the MP4 eclipsed any previous McLaren for sheer quality of manufacture. It was, admittedly, only powered by a Cosworth-Ford V8 at a time when the turbo revolution was gathering momentum, but Dennis had an eye firmly focussed on the future. For now, establishing the new team as a competitive force was the main priority.

Alain Prost had partnered John Watson during that final year of the old Team McLaren regime in 1980, but the young Frenchman cut and ran to Renault at the end of the year, disenchanted after a couple of major chassis breakages on the M29 which had pitched him into major accidents. This effectively saved Watson's bacon, for, after two disappointing seasons struggling with

the uncompetitive chassis, Mayer felt his determination and commitment were in question.

Prost's abrupt switch gave John the chance to restore his tarnished reputation, partnered in '81 by the erratic Marlboro-backed novice Andrea de Cesaris who crashed far too often for Dennis' peace of mind. Happily, the steady Watson scored the team's first win, surging the MP4 through into first place at Silverstone as Rene Arnoux's Renault RE30 faded with engine trouble to record a memorable British Grand Prix victory. Dennis had promised Marlboro a single victory in McLaren International's maiden season. Now he could breathe again.

For 1982, Dennis lured twice World Champion Niki Lauda out of retirement and, while the team would continue with Cosworth-Ford engines for the time being, began to lay plans for the team's own turbocharged engine. Dennis had always been one to think big and, with Barnard earning a reputation as an engineering perfectionist, it was always unlikely that they would be satisfied with any of the existing, first generation turbos.

At the end of 1981, Ron Dennis had asked Porsche whether it would consider designing and building him a state-of-the-art turbocharged Grand Prix engine on a pure commercial basis, with McLaren footing the bill. Barnard laid down his own stringent design parameters and, as the result of his deliberations with Hans Mezger, chief of the Porsche engine design unit, the German company's Research and Development department produced an 80-degree twin-turbo V6 with all its pumps and other

ancillaries at the front of the block, the better to integrate the end product into a ground effect chassis.

The first McLaren-commissioned, Porsche V6 was ready to run on the test bed in December 1982, six weeks after FISA burst the bombshell that flat-bottomed cars would be mandatory from the start of 1983, thereby partly compromising Barnard's vision of the ideal ground-effect engine configuration. But the Porsche V6 project pressed ahead and Dennis cast around for a backer to finance the 'production run' of engines necessary to go racing.

The Franco-Saudi high technology company Techniques d'Avant Garde (TAG), already a sponsor of the Williams team, agreed to take up the financial challenge and a new company, TAG Turbo Engines, was established in partnership with McLaren International. This more or less coincided with Dennis buying out the shareholdings of both Teddy Mayer and Tyler Alexander to take control of McLaren International, while Mansour Ojjeh, son of TAG founder Akram Ojjeh, would join him as a significant shareholder soon afterwards.

Meanwhile, throughout 1982, McLaren won four Grands Prix with their Cosworth-engined cars. Lauda triumphed at Long Beach and Brands Hatch, Watson at Zolder and in the new Detroit street race. The following year, in the Cosworth car's twilight, only Watson would win, at Long Beach. The first TAG turbo prototype was fielded at Zandvoort and two cars raced for the balance of the year, Lauda climbing to second place at Kyalami before electrical problems intervened.

Many observers regarded that showing in South Africa as a

Left: Frustrating moment for Prost as Senna laps him during the 1989 Mexican Grand Prix.

Right: Senna (*top*) remained the man to beat into 1989, his victory in the rain-soaked Belgian Grand Prix at Spa (*bottom*) confirming his pre-eminence in the wet.

Championship in a typically dynamic drive through the field to victory in the Japanese Grand Prix at Suzuka after stalling on the starting grid, but generally the two men were extremely well matched throughout the year. The Honda turbo V6 engines displayed a remarkable blend of reliability, economy and power, splendidly complimented by their two top class drivers.

McLaren and Honda sought to sustain this level of excellence in 1989 with the advent of the post-turbo era, Honda's RA109E 3.5-litre V10 engine again managing to outclass the field. But the personal relationship between Prost and Senna became progressively less tenable as the season wore on, and although the team notched up ten wins to clinch the Constructors' title, and Prost became Drivers' champion, it was a tense and unhappy period in the team's history. The drivers seldom spoke to each other, Honda became extremely annoyed at Prost's implications that they were favouring Senna in terms of engines, and the title battle ended with a collision between the two cars at Suzuka, under the noses of the Honda big guns.

The 1989 season ended with Senna being unjustly pilloried by FISA for dangerous driving, a $100,000 fine and a six month's suspended ban adding to his disappointment over losing the Championship crown to his team-mate and arch-rival. Yet despite all these political and personal problems, McLaren International remained the team to beat into 1990 even though Alain Prost had decided to move on and join Nigel Mansell in the Ferrari line-up.

Lotus in Decline

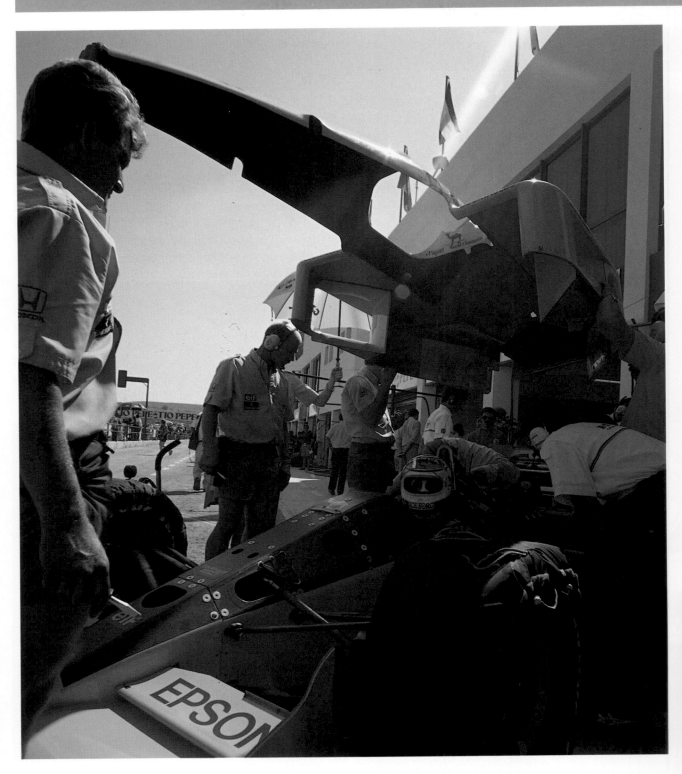

Left: Final preparations for Piquet's car before the 1988 Spanish GP.

Right: Nakajima in action, Spain 1988.

Below: Piquet during the same race.

Below left: Ayrton Senna kept up morale through 1985 with some superb performances in the Lotus 97T-Renault.

In '86, Senna really had stemmed Team Lotus' decline superbly, motivating the entire workforce in a manner nobody could really recall since the heyday of Mario Andretti eight years earlier. The Brazilian was prepared to give 110 per cent effort in a manner that Colin Chapman would have loved, and all his engineers and mechanics responded magnificently. Although Senna's eight pole positions translated into a mere two race victories (at Jerez and Detroit), a succession of good finishes kept him in play for the World Championship until the last race of the European season.

However, despite Renault's best effort with the special 'DP' version of its powerful EF15bis V6 engine, the Anglo-French partnership could not match Williams and Honda when it came to balancing power output with the requisite frugal fuel consumption under the new 195-litre fuel restrictions, the introduction of which had been postponed from 1985. The 'DP' label stood for *Distribution Pneumatique*, a system which used compressed air to close the valves thereby eliminating the need for valve springs.

The reduction in reciprocating mass allowed these latest engines to be run up to 12,500rpm, as against the earlier engines' limit of 11,000rpm, but by the middle of the year Senna was understandably anxious to try a Honda V6. A deal was done to secure the Japanese engines for Team Lotus' 1987 programme, although this involved taking on the journeyman Satoru Nakajima as number two driver. The team also forged its Honda programme round the use of the computer-controlled 'active' suspension which had been in the early stages of its development at the time of Chapman's death.

As things transpired, the added weight of the active suspension system allied to the inferior aerodynamics of the Lotus 99T as compared with the Williams FW11B, conspired yet again to blunt Senna's challenge throughout the 1987 season. The

Above: Joyous celebration after the 1985 Grand Prix of Europe, Nigel's first Formula 1 victory.

Left: Mansell came closest to the Championship at the wheel of the Williams-Honda FW11 during 1986.

Bottom left: Surfing through the rain at Monaco, 1984, in the Lotus 95T, Nigel crashed out while leading.

Right: His first helping of Championship points came with this third place in Belgium, 1981, driving the Lotus 81.

Angelis and an early third place in that season's Belgian Grand Prix did a great deal for his image and enthusiasm. His personal relationship with Chapman strengthened over the ensuing couple of seasons, but he had a less-than-successful relationship with Lotus team manager Peter Warr who rejoined the Hethel outfit in time for the '82 season. Consequently, after Chapman's sudden death in December 1982, Nigel found himself in a rather uncomfortable environment.

The results took a long time to come. In 1981 and 82 he could only manage 14th place in the Championship, in 1983 he was 12th and in 1984 ninth. By the time he quit Team Lotus to join Williams, as partner to Keke Rosberg, he had yet to improve on that third place finish he had achieved at Zolder in the early months of his fulltime F1 career. That said, in 1984 he overtook Alain Prost's McLaren to lead the rain-soaked Monaco Grand Prix in the Renault turbo-engined Lotus 95T, only to throw away potential victory with a slide into a barrier, and also qualified superbly on pole position at Dallas.

By this stage, Mansell had developed something of a reputation as a disruptive influence within Team Lotus and Rosberg was openly alarmed when the news broke that Nigel would be joining him in the Williams-Honda squad. The Finn asked for a release from his contract, which Frank Williams understandably declined, but Keke would later concede that this had been an over-reaction. Once his initial caution had been overcome, Keke confessed to liking Nigel a great deal.

Joining Williams was the crucial catalyst which helped propel Nigel Mansell to stardom. At the wheel of the Williams-Honda FW10 he finally broke his F1 duck by winning the Grand Prix of Europe at Brands Hatch, following that up immediately with another triumph in the next race, the South African Grand Prix at Kyalami. But by the time Mansell hit his winning streak, Rosberg had decided to switch to McLaren for 1986, replacing the retiring Niki Lauda as Prost's team-mate. Replacing him at Williams was Brabham refugee Nelson Piquet.

The superb new Williams FW11-Honda was destined to be the

Left: Nigel storming to victory at Montreal in the 1986 Canadian Grand Prix.

Below left: Ferrari man for 1989. Nigel in the type 640 during the Italian Grand Prix.

Right: Richie Ginther gave Honda their first F1 win with the transverse V12-engined 1½-litre machine in 1965.

Bottom right: John Surtees with the 3-litre Honda V12. It was a difficult partnership, but yielded victory in the 1967 Italian Grand Prix.

Unabashed, Mansell repeated his onslaught in 1987, the uprated 'B' version of the Williams-Honda FW11 proving just as formidable a tool. And again, team-mate Piquet was the man to beat. In the event, Nigel won the San Marino, French, British, Austrian, Spanish and Mexican Grands Prix only to crash heavily in practice for the inaugural Japanese Grand Prix at Suzuka, injuring his back badly enough to non-start in both that event and the final race in Adelaide. His misfortune handed the less spectacular Piquet the Championship, the Brazilian having concentrated on consistently gathering points rather than always aiming for race wins.

Williams was to be rewarded for fumbling the '86 drivers' Championship by losing its supply of Honda engines for 1988, but Mansell's unquenchable commitment took the Judd-engined FW12 to fine second places at Silverstone (behind Senna) and Jerez (behind Prost), highlights of a troubled season in which he decided to join Ferrari for 1989.

At the wheel of the ambitious new John Barnard-designed Ferrari 640, complete with its novel electro-hydraulic seven speed transmission, Mansell cemented his partnership with the famous Italian team by winning on his debut outing in Rio. That ensured his deification in Italy aided by his subsequent victory in Hungary, where he became the only man all season to beat Ayrton Senna's McLaren-Honda MP4/5 in a straight fight. Later he would be disqualified from the Portuguese Grand Prix for reversing in the pit lane during a routine tyre stop, a subsequent collision with Senna after apparently ignoring the black flag earning him a one-race suspension from the following week's Spanish Grand Prix.

These hiccups notwithstanding, Mansell finished his first season at Ferrari with his personal reputation considerably enhanced. He was driving better than ever and, despite having established himself as one of the sport's top earners, showed no signs of losing the sharp cutting edge of his commitment and determination.

car of the year, but when Piquet ran away with the first race of the season in front of his home crowd at Rio, he could perhaps have been forgiven for thinking that his third World Championship would be little more than a formality. After all, Mansell had shown his old streak of impetuosity tangling with Senna's Lotus 98T on the opening lap of the Brazilian race, so the Englishman was clearly going to be easy meat.

Nothing could have been further from the truth. Mansell knew he was approaching the absolute zenith of his racing form and proved it dramatically with superb victories in the Belgian, Canadian, French, British and Portuguese Grands Prix. Only a tyre failure in the closing stages of the Australian Grand Prix at Adelaide prevented him from grasping the World Championship crown he was now so qualified to wear.

The Sun Rises

Honda first became involved in F1 back in 1964 when it fielded a 1½-litre, transverse V12-engined F1 prototype as a prelude to a serious Championship assault the following season. Richie Ginther scored the marque's first success when he won the 1965 Mexican Grand Prix, the final race of the 1½-litre F1, and Honda continued into the new 3-litre F1 with a brand new V12.

Former World Champion John Surtees was recruited to drive for the team in 1967, winning the Italian Grand Prix by a length from Jack Brabham's Brabham-Repco in a sensational finish. Disappointingly, this victory was not to signal future success, and the 1968 season produced both disappointment and tragedy when Jo Schlesser was killed in the revolutionary air-cooled RA302 when it crashed during the opening stages of the French Grand Prix. The team then withdrew from F1 at the end of that season.

Honda's long road back to F1 began in 1981 when the Japanese company renewed an involvement with Ralt boss Ron Tauranac, providing a 2-litre, 80-degree V6 iron-block F2 engine for his team to use in the European Championship series. Honda had previously enjoyed a very cordial relationship with Tauranac in the days of the 1-litre Brabham-Hondas which ruled the F2 roost in 1966. The 2-litre V6 proved highly successful and Honda took its first step into the world of 1½-litre turbocharged F1 by initiating a pilot programme with the Spirit team at the start of 1983.

Swedish driver Stefan Johansson, already one of Spirit's F2 drivers, was signed up to drive this development car which contested the non-title Race of Champions and then joined the Championship trail in time for the British Grand Prix at Silverstone. But at the end of August, Honda announced a long-term deal with Williams and Frank's team had its first FW09s ready for Keke Rosberg and Jacques Laffite to handle in the final race of the season, the South African Grand Prix at Kyalami.

Honda had literally supplied the basic engines and their turbochargers, leaving it Williams to work out an exhaust system and intercooler layout. With less than optimum cooling, Rosberg reported that the Honda short-stroke RA168-E V6 felt an extremely pleasant and progressive engine at first acquaintance. Into the 1984 season, improved intercooling allowed them to run more boost and, suddenly, the peaky and spectacular power delivery snapped the FW09s from initial understeer to massive oversteer. Rosberg, never one to hide his light under a bushel, blamed a flexing chassis for the problem, much to the acute irritation of Williams' designer Patrick Head, but still managed to squeeze a memorable victory at Dallas out of the Williams-Honda combination.

In truth, the engine needed a lot of work. Its cylinder block was insufficiently rigid and it was prone to overheating on one

bank of cylinders. Later in the '84 season, an attempt to squeeze more power from a wider performance band was rewarded with nothing but a host of major, piston-related engine failures. Thankfully, Honda's F1 director Nobuhiko Kawamoto understood the complexities and vagaries of the motor racing business, having worked as a mechanic on the F2 Brabham-Hondas almost twenty years earlier. He directed another engineering team in the company's research and development department to come up with a solution.

By 1985, with a more useable power curve, better heat control and improved fuel consumption, the 'E' specification version of

the V6 was fitted, from the Canadian Grand Prix onwards, to the first Williams carbon fibre composite chassis, the FW10. The Williams-Honda alliance was really showing signs of coming good, Rosberg duly winning through the streets of Detroit the week after a fourth place at Montreal.

By the end of the season a revised aerodynamic package on the FW10, taking advantage of specially-made lower inlet manifolding for the engine, was introduced in time for the Grand Prix of Europe at Brands Hatch. As history relates, Nigel Mansell raced to a memorable first F1 success, following that up with a splendid triumph in South Africa. With Keke rounding off the year in Adelaide, winning his last race for the team before switching to McLaren for '86, the Williams-Honda partnership looked in splendid shape for 1986.

By the end of the '85 season, the Honda V6 turbo was nudging the production-block BMW M12/13 in terms of ultimate power output, but the German engine was by this time beset with horrifying reliability problems. Mobil, the Williams team's contracted fuel sponsor, had meanwhile done a superb job developing a toluene-based high aromatic fuel. In conjunction with Honda's own highly efficient engine management system, this enabled the 1986 specification engine to develop around 950bhp in race trim (at 4-bar boost pressure) and a maximum of 1120bhp when wound up to 5-bar for banzai qualifying runs.

The very personal, deep collaboration implicit in this Anglo-Japanese relationship was emphasised by the way in which Honda established a lavishly equipped race shop adjacent to the team's Didcot factory. The new 195-litre Williams FW11 promised to be a huge improvement over the FW10 and, with Nelson Piquet joining Mansell in the driver line-up, the Brazilian's home victory at Rio on his maiden outing with the team was the prelude to a fabulously successful season.

Above left: Stefan Johansson with the Spirit-Honda during the 1983 British Grand Prix.

Left: Nigel Mansell's Williams FW10 wins the Grand Prix of Europe just over two years later.

Above: Keke Rosberg was a determined campaigner in the Williams-Honda, winning at Detroit with the FW10 in 1985.

Right: The previous year he had given the Anglo-Japanese partnership its maiden win at Dallas with the FW09.

Ironically, for all Piquet's early optimism, 1986 proved to be the season in which Nigel Mansell came brilliantly to maturity, winning no fewer than five Grands Prix to Piquet's four. The two men went into the last race of the season each able to win the Drivers' Championship, their combined efforts long since having secured the Constructors' title for Williams and Honda. yet, somehow, through circumstance, bad luck, shortage of team discipline and, crucially in Mansell's case, a blown tyre, they allowed the title to slip through their fingers into the grasp of McLaren's Alain Prost.

Yet there was one key person missing throughout the 1986 season, a man whose presence at the pit wall might just conceivably have changed things. Returning from the final pre-season test session at the Circuit Paul Ricard, Frank Williams had sustained serious injuries in a car crash and was left paralysed from the waist down and confined to a wheelchair. His fight back to some semblance of normality occupied him for the entire season.

Many people believe, when Honda subsequently pulled the plug on their partnership with Williams at the end of August 1987, that the Japanese company did so because it was dissatisfied with the outcome of the '86 Drivers' Championship battle. Others suspected that the Honda management felt in some way uncomfortable dealing with a company run by a paraplegic. Either way, Williams Grand Prix Engineering would bounce back to prove that there was Life After Honda.

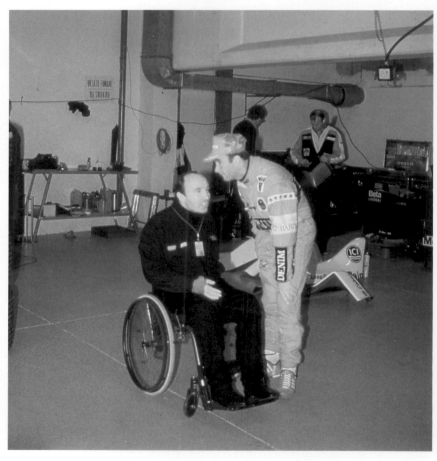

BMW and Unlimited Boost

The advent of the turbo era did not simply alter the technical challenge in Grand Prix racing, it also heralded a fundamental change in the structure of the sport. Since the late 1950s, Formula 1 had been the almost exclusive province of the special builder, the small specialist teams such as Lotus, Brabham and McLaren who built their challenge round 'proprietary' racing engines from Coventry Climax to Cosworth Engineering.

Even Ferrari and BRM, who prided themselves on making their own engines, were only one step up from this small specialist level. They may have appeared to be giant empires by the standards of the smaller teams, but were tiny when measured against the big international car manufacturing companies. It was really only in the 1980s that the full force of Fiat's technological support began to underpin the Ferrari team's efforts. By then, the technical stakes had been raised dramatically by the arrival of Renault, BMW, Honda and Porsche on a suddenly invigorated F1 scene.

While the evidence is that Renault's challenge may have been slightly blunted by the French team's policy of building its own chassis in addition to pursuing an engine development programme, BMW and Honda wisely adopted a different course. The complexities of turbo engine development were such that they chose to forge a partnership with an established, top-line British F1 team who could provide instant access to state-of-the-art chassis technology.

BMW shrewdly came to an arrangement with Bernie Ecclestone's Brabham team and based its F1 programme round a production car engine, its single turbo version of the M12/13 four-cylinder unit first appearing during practice for the 1981 British Grand Prix at Silverstone. At that time, Nelson Piquet was mid-

way through his first World Championship challenge at the wheel of his Cosworth-engined Brabham BT49C and, as things turned out, the BMW turbocar would not be raced before the start of the following season.

By the time BMW moved into F1 action, Renault had well and truly gone on to the defensive, Alfa Romeo was laying plans for a V8, Honda had plans to produce a turbo version of its 1½-litre V6 and McLaren had commissioned Porsche to build a tailor-made, state-of-the-art twin-turbo V6 which would owe nothing to any existing engine. Ferrari, of course, were well established with a wide-angle, 120-degree twin-turbo V6, which made its race

Above left: Nelson Piquet's Williams FW11 leads Ayrton Senna's Lotus 98T during the 1986 Hungarian Grand Prix.

Left: Frank Williams in conversation with Nigel Mansell.

Above right: Nelson Piquet in the 1982 Brabham-BMW BT50.

Right: The BMW four-cylinder M12/13 single turbo engine installed in the Brabham BT50.

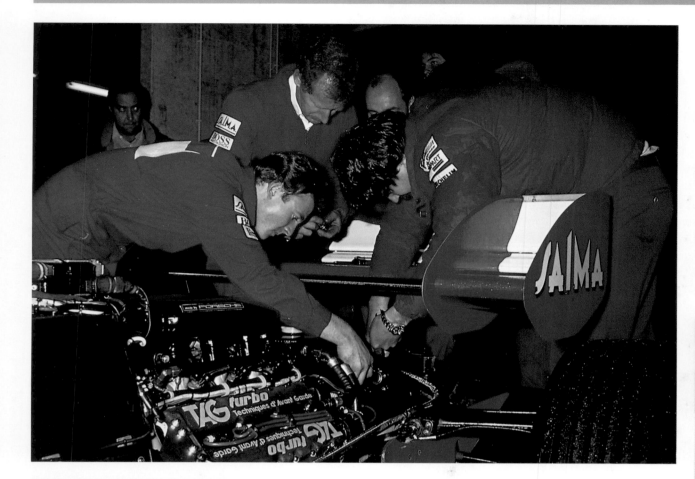

Left: The Porsche-made, TAG V6 engine raised F1 turbo technology to fresh heights at the start of 1984.

Bottom left: Alfa Romeo tried a 1½-litre turbo V8; it proved consistently disappointing.

Below: Turbos ahead. The start of the 1982 Austrian Grand Prix at the Osterreichring, with the Brabham-BMWs of Piquet and Patrese wheel-to-wheel with the Renaults of Prost and Arnoux at the front of the field.

Racing as a Business

From its earliest days, Grand Prix racing has always attracted enormous crowds, a blend of novelty value and sheer spectacle guaranteeing its position as one of the most dramatic of international sports. Yet, in the four decades since World War Two, we have come to live in a rather blasé world where high technology achievements of breathtaking proportions are taken for granted. In 1969, for example, America put the first man on the moon. By contrast, a Formula 1 battle at Silverstone between Jackie Stewart and Jochen Rindt looked pretty small beer.

Moreover, television coverage of sporting events was becoming ever more sophisticated and wide-ranging. Formula 1 racing could not remain the last bastion of conservatism, drawing its financial backing only from traditional paymasters such as the tyre and fuel companies, if it was to flourish in such an enlightened age. Starting grids had to be fuller, facilities had to be considerably improved and the sport's entire image up-graded. If Grand Prix racing was going to be a major international business, it had to have as much of a cachet as Wimbledon, the Henley Regatta or the Derby. The mud, thermos-flask and stale sandwiches image of the average race track had to be buried, once and for all, if Formula 1 was to have a chance.

Enter, once more to our story, Bernard Ecclestone. Throughout the 1970s, in his role as President of the Formula One Constructors' Association, he made race organisers squeal with his financial demands. In a relatively short space of time, FOCA's prize fund requirements doubled, and then doubled again. By 1976, the prize fund for the British Grand Prix had risen to £258,000, almost double that paid out by the Brands Hatch organisers four years earlier. At the time it seemed a brutalising affair, as if Bernie was pursuing a get-rich-quick, short-term policy. In fact, it was quite the reverse.

Ecclestone rightly concluded that most race organisers were failing to maximise the promotional potential of their events. He also firmly estimated that the sport's popularity was such as to sustain a major price increase. In 1976 the Brands Hatch organisers held their breath, doubled the admission prices and found that Ecclestone's judgement had been correct. The attendance figure was not adversely affected.

Pushing hard for such an increased financial commitment from individual race organisers meant, of course, that the Constructors too became obliged to strengthen their obligations. Ecclestone identified that one of Grand Prix racing's weakest

Above left: A sea of sponsored caps and shirts in one of today's F1 grandstands helps get the message across.

Left: Gold Leaf girls with Lotus driver Emerson Fittipaldi at the 1971 British Grand Prix. This cigarette sponsorship was F1's first, starting in 1968.

Above: Strategically placed sponsor identification on the winner's podium is expensive, but guarantees television exposure.

Right: Huge advertising hoardings dwarf the cars at Imola. But they get the sponsors' message across.

Left: Monaco in 1964 with only a handful of advertising banners, mainly industry-related.

Below: Durex (a well-known brand of contraceptive in Britain) sponsorship of Team Surtees provided plenty of controversy – and coverage – during the mid-1970s.

Right: Expensive exposure – a decal on Alain Prost's helmet can cost hundreds of thousands of dollars.

aspects was its inconsistency in regard to providing full fields for race organisers.

In the days of the pre-FOCA package deal, it had been the habit for race organisers to negotiate individually with the various teams. If a particular team did not like the deal which was being offered, and was unable to coax the organiser into paying more, then it was free to stay away. Ferrari had gained a particularly poor reputation in this respect, for example, missing the British Grands Prix in 1960 and 66 for spurious reasons, the former occasion at a time when it had an English driver leading the team in the form of Tony Brooks. Clearly, this just would not do.

From 1974 onwards, membership of the Formula One Constructors' Association accorded a team a guaranteed start in every race – and a binding obligation to contest every round of the Championship. This was an extremely positive development, ensuring that every race organiser knew precisely how many cars would be competing from the start of the year. This development was followed by a permanent numbering system, whereby competitors retained the same racing numbers from year to year, only the incoming and outgoing World Champions and their team-mates exchanging placings to ensure that, in line with established custom, the reigning title-holder carried 'number one'.

Ecclestone's endeavours brought an air of consistency and predictability to the Grand Prix scene, albeit at a considerable price to race organisers. But FOCA was always prepared to enter a financial partnership with those race organisers who were worried about the potential profitability of their event. In some cases, the Constructors even took over the responsibility for staging the entire event, occasionally even losing money.

Whatever criticisms Ecclestone's impatiently autocratic endeavours may have attracted over the years – and there were many – FOCA steered Grand Prix racing along a highly profitable and commercially sound course which, during the 1980s, was rewarded with a dramatic expansion of television coverage to all corners of the world. The sporting purist may have winced at such a strategy, but changing times demand a changing approach and Ecclestone was never afraid of the enterprising solution.

The McLaren-Hondas, Prost and Senna

It is always something of a gamble when a top-line team selects two absolute aces to drive its cars, but the possibility of personal tension has to be set against the obligation to maximise that team's winning potential. Mercedes-Benz, Vanwall, Lotus and Williams all chose to recruit two top-line drivers at one time or another, but, during the 1980s, McLaren came to regard it as an absolute fundamental cornerstone of their F1 philosophy.

Ever since Alain Prost and Niki Lauda between them won 12 out of the 1984 season's 16 World Championship rounds, the logic of having the two best drivers in the world became lodged in the mind of McLaren boss Ron Dennis. After all, having expended vast sums of money and engineering effort to field highly competitive racing cars, it was natural that they should each be given the best chance of success. But pairing the best in the business could have an unexpectedly irritating downside, as Dennis and the McLaren team would find to their discomfort in 1989.

Alain Prost had spent his first year in F1 driving for McLaren during 1980, but was not happy with the team's level of mechanical reliability and switched to Renault for three seasons from the start of 1981. He was then unjustly forced to carry the can for the French team's failure to win the 1983 Championship, but, within days of being shown the door, found himself snapped up again by McLaren to partner Niki Lauda for the 1984 season. The Frenchman would continue to win two World Championships in their TAG turbo-engined cars (1985 and 86), establishing himself as the most statistically successful F1 driver of all time by the end of 1987 when he scored his 28th career victory, beating Jackie Stewart's 13-year-old record of 27 wins.

For 1988, McLaren had forged a deal with Honda for the supply of its RA168E 1½-litre V6 turbocharged engines and Brazilian driver Ayrton Senna left Lotus to drive alongside Prost. In this year of transitional technical regulations, the new McLaren MP4/4 chassis powered by the outgoing Honda turbos, even constrained within the 2.5-bar/150-litre regulations which prevailed in '88, exercised a level of domination that allowed Prost and Senna to make the Championship battle their own personal affair.

From the outset, the two men faced subtly differing challenges. Senna had already spent a year working in conjunction with the Honda technicians, yet he was new to the McLaren ranks. Prost, sitting tenant and totally familiar with the working of the team, now had to forge a working relationship with the formal, cautious Japanese. An objective analysis of events suggests that Senna was more successful integrating himself into the McLaren team than Prost was infiltrating the Honda set-up. Certainly Senna proved the quicker driver, yet he took more risks. Prost was more dependable, but just could not get through traffic like his younger team-mate and displayed a deep-seated aversion toward racing in the rain.

Prost kicked off with a win in Rio. In fact, he won three out of

Above: Prost leads Senna in a McLaren-Honda 1-2 at the start of the 1988 French Grand Prix.

Left: Team-mates and talking, for the moment at least. Prost and Senna with the McLaren MP4/4 at Montreal, 1988.

Above right: Alain Prost closes in on Senna during the 1988 French Grand Prix.

Right: Senna looks on impassively while Honda engineers check his engine.

the first four races, adding Mexico and Monaco (where Senna crashed while leading) to his tally. At Imola, Senna simply ran away to win the San Marino race. On the one hand it looked as though the Championship would be secured on wins alone, but sometimes it seemed as though the outcome would be resolved by freak accidents and incidents.

When Senna wiped a corner off against a barrier when leading Monaco by a huge margin, the sages predicted that this could be the day he would rue if he failed to win the Championship. Similarly, Prost's withdrawal from the sodden British Grand Prix at Silverstone, a race won brilliantly by Ayrton, might come to be regarded as his personal Waterloo.

After that shaky start, Senna counter-attacked ferociously. He won Canada and Detroit, was beaten by Alain at Paul Ricard, then took four straight wins at Silverstone, Hockenheim, Hungaroring and Spa-Francorchamps. Alain, who rashly

made an incorrect aerodynamic adjustment to his car just prior to the start of the Belgian race, virtually conceded the Championship at the post-race press conference. He did not know how he could catch Senna.

Trends change, though, and suddenly it appeared there might be a way for Prost. Monza proved a disaster for both of them, Prost succumbing to engine trouble while Senna tripped over novice Jean-Louis Schlesser as he sought to fend off Berger's fast-rising Ferrari going into the penultimate lap. The Frenchman, deputising for an unwell Nigel Mansell at the wheel of the Williams-Judd FW12, proved just as adamant as Ayrton that the incident was not his fault.

Prost could now see an outside chance. He won the Portuguese Grand Prix at Estoril, Senna almost squeezing him into the pit wall as the Frenchman swooped by into the lead at the end of the opening lap. It was an incident which caused a fleeting degree of tension between the two drivers, although it was to look like kid's stuff compared with what was to follow in 1989. Prost then won at Jerez against the odds, conserving his fuel with remarkable skill, but Senna came back to clinch the title in front of Honda's home crowd at Suzuka, slashing back to win brilliantly on a rain-slicked track surface after stalling at the start, but just managing to bump start his McLaren into life. You don't get many second chances like that in a Grand Prix career.

Prost rounded off the season with a win in Australia, the balance of wins tipped eight/seven in favour of the Brazilian, although the convoluted points scoring system, which counted only the best eleven scores, saw Prost, who had more points overall than Senna, lose this advantage when the rule was applied.

By the late summer of 1988, Honda's new naturally aspirated RA109E V10-cylinder engine was undergoing extensive testing in preparation for the new naturally aspirated F1 which finally consigned the turbos to the history books at the start of the 1989

Championship. Yet again, Senna and Prost would confidently assume the role of Grand Prix pacemakers, yet their personal relationship would degenerate dramatically.

The problem started at Imola, prior to the second round of the championship. Senna, whose Brazilian Grand Prix chances had been wiped out by his involvement in a first corner collision, proposed a 'no passing' arrangement on the first lap. The race was stopped and re-started after Gerhard Berger crashed heavily in his Ferrari, and although Prost got away first, Ayrton overtook going into the braking area for the first uphill left-hander.

The precise interpretation of who said what when, and what did it all mean anyway, preoccupied both drivers for the next few weeks. Prost accused Senna of being unprincipled. Senna kept his peace, but later went on record as saying he could not understand what all the fuss was about, venturing the view that it 'wasn't his fault that Prost was screwed in the head.' The two men conducted the remainder of the season without speaking to each other. It was an extremely childish situation which both drivers got away with only thanks to their considerable ability behind the wheel.

Prost later added fuel to the flames by suggesting that Honda had been less-than-impartial when it came to supplying equal

Left: Senna used Honda power to win the 1987 Monaco Grand Prix for Lotus. By the time he arrived at McLaren he had forged a close bond with the Japanese technicians.

Below left: Senna leads Prost in the controversial 1989 San Marino Grand Prix. The turbo era now over, their cars are powered by Honda's radical new V10-cylinder 3.5-litre engine.

Right: Delight shows on Senna's face after a close victory in the 1988 Hungarian Grand Prix.

Left: Alain Prost, McLaren's most prolific winning driver.

Below: The view the opposition got of Alain's McLaren-Honda during the 1989 French Grand Prix.

Right: Two of the new breed of 3.5-litre F1 engines from Ford (top) and Renault are set to challenge Honda in the future.

engines. However, Senna kept his lips firmly sealed when his MP4/5 retired due to mechanical problems in four consecutive races; Phoenix, Montreal, Paul Ricard and Silverstone.

Honda countered Prost's allegations by hinting that his delicate throttle operation, which had been such an integral part of his success conserving fuel with the 1988 turbo car, now prevented him from getting the best out of the high-revving naturally aspirated V10. Senna, on the other hand, had a throttle-blipping style which was better suited to an atmospheric engine than a turbo running on a restricted quota of fuel.

Either way, the battle for supremacy raged right through to the Japanese Grand Prix at Suzuka where, after two seasons of allowing himself to be intimidated into making room for his team-mate, Prost, who by this stage had signed for Ferrari for 1990, made it clear that he would be leaving no gaps on this occasion. Thus, from the moment the Frenchman surged into the lead at the start from second place on the grid, Senna had a major problem on his hands.

Prost was driving brilliantly, matching every quick lap Ayrton could pull from the bag. Both had perfect tyre stops and, with a handful of laps to go, Senna knew he would have to take a risk if he was to keep his Championship chances open. Duly, he did so, lunging down the inside of Prost with two wheels on the grass as the two cars scrabbled into the tight chicane before the pits. Alain, true to his word, turned into Senna's car and the Championship battle was over.

Senna regained the track, via the chicane escape road, to be first past the chequered flag, yet he was disqualified and victory awarded to Alessandro Nannini in the Benetton-Ford B189. McLaren took the matter to the FISA Court of Appeal where the whole matter took on an uncomfortably complex dimension as

the sport's governing body raked up a host of irrelevant accusations which left McLaren feeling that it had no alternative but to seek legal redress in the civil courts.

Thus ended one of the most turbulent, yet successful, driving partnerships in Grand Prix history. Both men firmly believed their own personal behaviour had been correct and the other's severely lacking. Yet both drivers were consumate politicians in their own right, Prost's easy charm wooing the media, while Senna's behind-the-scenes diplomacy ensured that he achieved a very special relationship with both McLaren and Honda which, in his view, was all that mattered.

Where Next for the Grand Prix?

By the start of the 1990s, Jean-Marie Balestre would claim that there were a total of twenty 3.5-litre engines either competing in F1 or waiting in the wings for the right moment to launch their challenge on the Grand Prix scene. However optimistic that assessment is shown to be in years to come, there is no doubt that the FISA Formula 1 World Championship is now firmly established as one of the most highly publicised of international sports, benefitting from enormous media and television coverage to a level exceeded only by the Olympic Games and the World Cup.

As a technological showcase, the end of the turbo era has returned engine development to a path more in tune with contemporary road car engineering. Multi-valve, naturally aspirated engines which develop power efficiently and economically have become a priority for the world's motor industry as we enter the last decade of this century, so it is reassuring that international Grand Prix racing is providing a worthwhile lead in this respect.

The experiences of the past decade suggest that Grand Prix racing will have to fight even harder for its share of international television viewing figures over the years to come. Since the sport's financial security has grown increasingly to depend on such television coverage, future developments are likely to be attuned to sustaining this situation.

From the standpoint of the technical regulations, the one

Left: Nelson Piquet's 1989 Lotus-Judd advertising Camel cigarette sponsorship. But how long before legislation bans such sponsorship from the television screen?

Below left: Honda's splendid RA109E 3.5-litre V10 cylinder engine. The Japanese company has raised the technical stakes in F1 to hitherto undreamt-of levels.

Right: Nigel Mansell, his overalls dripping in sponsorship decals during his days with Williams, proving that the driver is still the single most important, identifiable, aspect of the entire business.

thing that FISA can do to attract new participants is to ensure the basic engine capacity rules remain stable for many years. The success of the 3-litre naturally aspirated F1, introduced in 1966, was so overwhelming that the category would almost certainly have remained in existence to this day had not Renault taken advantage of a loophole in its provisions to spark the turbo revolution in 1977. The investment in engine technology is these days so overwhelming that no manufacturer will commit itself without assurances that the rules are not about to be changed, thereby rendering useless a costly development programme.

However, Grand Prix racing will be obliged to adapt to changes. Majority opinion suggests that tobacco sponsorship of televised sporting events, and their competitors, will be severely restricted or even curtailed altogether. For the past two decades, Formula 1 has benefitted enormously from the financial support of the Marlboro, John Player, Camel and Barclay cigarette brands. It would be a brave man who confidently predicted that these companies will be able to sustain such a prominent sponsorship role throughout the 1990s, so F1 budgets may have to come from other commercial organisations that can be sold the benefits of such global television exposure, as well as the advantages of an association with such a glamorous and competitive high technology sport.

As far as the cars themselves are concerned, they are unlikely to change much from a visual point of view, any more than they did between 1980 and 1990. But they will unquestionably become even lighter, more rigid and stronger, increasingly employing automatic transmission and computer-controlled suspension systems. Fuel consumption will be further reduced and I suspect the environmentalists will insist that noise levels be reduced at whatever races take place on tracks within close proximity to large urban areas.

There is no real reason why Formula 1 should not continue to thrive with ever-increasing vigour throughout the 1990s as a technological showpiece for the endeavours of the world's major motor manufacturers. On the face of it, the enthusiastic observer may have some difficulty imagining just who might come along to topple McLaren, Williams and Ferrari from their current pre-eminent positions, but there is always ambitious new talent waiting in the junior formulae for the opportunity to topple the Old Guard. In that respect too, international motor racing has seldom looked healthier.

Acknowledgments

The publisher would like to thank Donald Sommerville who edited this book, David Eldred who designed it and Maria Costantino who did the picture research. We would also like to thank the following individuals and agencies for the illustrations:
Allsport: 89(top), 125(below), 134(below), 160(top)./Photo: Pascal Rondeau: 129, 135(below), 142, 143(top), 152(below), 165, 170(both), 171(top)
Allsport/Agence Vandystat/ Photo: Bernard Asset: 128(both), 130-131, 133(below), 136(top), 139(top), 141, 145(both), 158(top), 160(below), 167(below), 171(below),

172(below)./Photo: Alain Patrice: 136(below)./Photo: Jean-marc Loubat: 169
Creative Planners: 143(below)
Geoffrey Goddard Collection: 6-7, 8(both), 9(both), 10(both), 11, 12(both), 13(both) 15(both), 16(both), 17, 18-19, 20(both), 21(both), 22(top), 23(both), 24-25, 26, 27(all 3), 28, 29, 30, 31(both), 32, 34, 35(both), 36(both), 37, 38, 39, 40, 41, 42, 43, 44, 45(both), 46, 47, 57(top), 59(top), 60(below right), 61(top), 63(below), 64(both), 65(top), 72, 75(both), 76-77, 79(both), 81(below), 86(top), 91(below), 122(top), 153(both), 161.
Andrew Morland: 33(both)
Mark Newcombe: 137(top),

146(both), 147(both), 148(top), 149(top), 156(below), 166(both), 167(top)
Phipps Photographic: 48-49, 50(both), 51, 52, 53(all 3), 54(both), 55(both), 56(below), 57(below), 58, 59(below), 60(top & below left), 61(below), 62, 63(top), 65(below), 66(all 3), 67(both), 68, 69(both), 70, 73(both), 74, 78, 80(both), 81(top), 82, 83(both), 84(below), 85(both), 86(center & below), 87(both), 88(both), 89(below), 90(both), 91(top), 92(both), 93(both), 94(all 3), 95(both), 96(all 3), 97(both), 98(both), 99(both), 100(both), 101(both), 102(both), 103, 104(both), 105(both), 106(both), 107(both), 108, 109(all 3), 110(both),

112(both), 113(both), 114, 115(all 3), 116, 117(both), 118, 119(both), 120, 121(both), 122(below), 123, 124(top), 125(both), 126, 132, 133(top), 137(below), 138(below), 139(below), 140(both), 144, 148(below), 149(below), 150(below), 151(both), 154(both), 155(both), 156(top), 157(both), 158(below), 159, 162(both), 163(both), 164(both), 168(both), 172(top), 173
Porsche (West Germany): 14(both), 22(below)
The Research House: 56(top), 84(top)
Zooom: 134(top), 135(top), 150(top), 152(top)